BINGE EATING DISORDER:

Breaking Up Your Toxic
Relationship With Food

Lauren Ryan

Table of Contents

Introduction

I t was one of those days when all I remembered was that I was a stressed out mess. I was mentally exhausted from juggling work with home life, with no energy leftover for self-care or enjoyment. I guess you could say that I was functioning on autopilot. All of my energy was taken up by going to work and keeping up with household responsibilities. There was nothing in reserve for joy at the end of the day. I hadn't yet learned how to self-soothe or developed any reliable, healthy coping mechanisms to use when I needed stress relief. That's where food came in.

Things might have been a little better if there had been time to rest on the weekends. But there wasn't. Weekends were for the errands I had put off all week to keep up with work. Oh, and let's not forget social dinners, birthday parties, and whatever else I had RSVP'd to in a state of at least mild sanity before even more work piled up. All my energy was swallowed up by an endless stream of responsibilities. Food was my only escape, the only way out of my jumbled brain for even a few minutes at a time.

Overall, I felt that I had lost control of my life. I was drowning, and I needed help. But I didn't know where to turn. I had an image in my mind of the woman I wanted to be, and she looked a lot like the woman I am now: confident, genuinely happy with her life, and looking forward to the future. I knew that woman existed somewhere deep inside me, but she was buried under heaps of responsibilities. I desperately wanted to find my way back to her. So I did.

My turning point came on an ordinary day. I was about to do the thing I told myself I would never do again. Two days ago, I told myself it was over. The next time I was tempted to comfort myself by over-eating, I would find the strength to stop myself. That day, I had eaten until my anxiety was obliterated. Then I headed straight to the bathtub to drown myself in tears: I was just so disgusted with myself.

Yet, this was my usual way of dealing with life. I didn't want to look at myself. I didn't want to see that all-too-familiar look on my face, the one I get when I talk myself into going downstairs and doing it all over again.

But that night, I walked over to the mirror and looked into it anyway. I said to my reflection, "Lauren, you've been good for two days. You can have one cup of gelato, and then you'll stop. It's fine." And then I was off to the kitchen. I swung open the door to the freezer, and there it was: a container of chocolate gelato. Chocolate and gelato. The two most sinful delights ever dreamed into existence. What human being could resist? Just looking at it made me feel instantly better.

We always had it. We would do anything to get it, including driving forty-five minutes to a remote convenience store in the middle of nowhere. It was the only place that offered that particular pleasure after dark. My husband and just about everyone else on the planet knew it would immediately cheer me up. Somehow, food had become more than just a quick fix for my bad feelings. Apparently, it was others' quick fix for my feelings, too.

My mouth was watering, but I felt guilty, too. In the past two days, I had managed to keep myself from binge eating. Two days may not sound like much to you, but it's all relative. For me, they were the hardest two days of my life. Back then, food was my only outlet, and I was under significant stress. Resisting my cravings for two days had been exhausting, but I had pulled it off.

"That's why you deserve a little reward, Lauren. You've earned it," I rationalized inwardly. I heaped the first glorious scoop onto my spoon. Usually, I ate straight from the container. But this time I very meticulously dished out two small, doughnut-hole sized scoops. There! That's it, I thought. I put the lid back on the container of gelato and shoved it back into the freezer as if the cold treat was on fire. Then I jumped and nearly fell backward.

My husband was standing in the doorway, observing me. "I thought you were on a diet," he said quietly.

"I'm only human," I snapped. "It's a little reward at the end of a long week."

A brief pregnant pause filled the room. "I thought I was supposed to stop you from eating that."

"But it's just a tiny scoop," I protested, meeting his eyes.

Here's where the plot turned. I wish I could tell you that my loving husband turned around and said, "I love you. Put that down and let's talk." Or even, "Put that down now or I'm calling your mom." What the hell, even, "Put that down, or I'm calling *my* mom," would have sufficed. But that's not what happened.

Instead, my husband gave a slight shrug of his shoulders and said, "Babe, just use the popcorn bowl like you always do. You know you're going to fill that thing twenty times." Then he turned and walked upstairs.

For a moment, my entire world was frozen. It took me a second to recover and process what I was feeling. There was no way to sugarcoat it: I was devastated. It wasn't because of what he said. The truth was, my husband had no idea what his offhand words meant to me. How could he know? I had never opened up to anyone about just how much binge eating had taken over my life, and how hard a battle I was fighting against it.

Sure, there were clues. Like my not-so-little (and, let's face it, not-so-secret) stashes of sweets hidden all over the house. (I even had a bag of M & M's in the laundry room at this point, although to be fair, he hadn't discovered them. Yet). But my husband had always laughed it off—the insensitive jerk. Still, I knew he had no idea how ashamed I was about my lack of control.

He probably forgot what he said less than thirty seconds after the words fell from his lips. But they would ring out in my mind for weeks to come. They marked a turning point in my life. That insensitive jerk was right, and I knew it. I was going to fill the bowl twenty times tonight. I wasn't going to have just one cup. I knew it when I had the ingenious idea of actually scooping my portion into a bowl like a normal person instead of eating from the container like a slob.

And then, I was going to feel so bad about the whole thing that I went downstairs and started it again. When my despair really hit rock bottom, I'd say something like this to myself: "Lauren, this is something you live with. Sure, it's a problem. But it's not like you're sticking a needle in your arm. Everyone has their vice." I would tell myself anything to convince myself that I wasn't killing myself slowly. But I was.

My husband had been right. And I was sick of him, or anyone else, being right about me. I wanted to show everyone, most of all, myself, that I was capable of starting over and changing my life. It wasn't easy, but I kept that promise to myself. I admitted to myself that I had Binge Eating Disorder and accepted it. I walked back upstairs, looked into the mirror, and said, "Lauren, you have Binge Eating Disorder. Tonight you're going to accept that. Tomorrow you are going to start dealing with your feelings about it. Most importantly, you are going to reach out for support and make the changes you've been dreaming about."

It was the first step toward self-love that I had made, and I'm proud of it to this day. I won't ever lie to you: my road to recovery had its share of ups and downs, and so will yours. Rock bottom is different for everyone, but mine came when I was so sick to death of overeating that I didn't even want to anymore. I knew I would be engaged in a long struggle against my urge to binge because it had become a deeply ingrained coping mechanism. But the temporary high that binge eating brought wasn't worth the long-term pain and risk to my health. I was not only harming my body systems and decreasing my longevity, but I was also slowly dying inside. I had reached a point where I was no longer experiencing my life; I was numbing the ups and downs of it with food. Any time I wasn't eating, I was stressed. Overeating had become my respite, and it was time to find another one. I knew I had to start within myself.

I broke up with binge eating that night. If you've ever broken up with a lover who tasted sweet but was ultimately toxic to you, then you have an idea of how I felt. I was done. The realization alone made me feel beautiful for the first time in longer than I could re-member. It had nothing to do with the way I looked, and everything to do with the way I felt about myself inside.

Guess what? I've been feeling beautiful ever since not because I haven't struggled with Binge Eat-ing Disorder, but because I kept my promise to my-self. Let me be clear: although I slowly adopted new, healthy eating patterns and changed my relationship with food for the better, my recovery was not about dietary restrictions. It was about shifting from a place of self-loathing to self-love. In the past, whenever I had the urge to eat my pain away, I always berated myself for it. This, of course, led to feelings of hope-lessness and low self-esteem. How did I deal with those feelings? I wasn't ready to process them, or where they came from, so I ate my feelings. I did it every day.

But after the night I decided to make a change, I no longer berated myself when stress built up, and the urge to binge took over. Instead, I took deep, calming breaths. I replaced the negative, critical voice in my head with a kind one. "Lauren, I know you haven't had an easy week. Your stress levels are off the charts. Why don't you sit down and choose from a list of healthier ways to deal with your feelings?"

After some time, it dawned on me that those words were almost exactly what I had longed to hear my husband say the night he encouraged me to use a bigger bowl, so I wouldn't fill it twenty times. (I know, major husband fail). But the truth is, I couldn't teach the people around me how I needed to be loved until I learned how to love myself.

Are you done feeling hopeless and out of control? I'm going to tell you something: being done is a choice, not just a feeling. We can feel fed up a million times, but keep going back for more. You have to make a conscious decision to break up your toxic relationship with food.

You have to look in the mirror like I did and say, "You can do this. You can be done with the addiction controlling you, and take back your life."

But it's impossible to do it alone. I wrote this book to provide you with a foundation of knowledge about Binge Eating Disorder and recovery, but I also wanted you to know that you're not alone. I have been where you are, and I took control of my life. Trust me, if I can do it, anyone can. But you have to be done. You have to make a commitment. It's the first step in a long but ultimately life-saving recovery process.

I am here to tell you that as long as you remain committed, it gets easier. And after a while, you'll notice that it's not just easier. You'll see that you're starting to feel better inside and out. It is entirely possible to feel free from fear in the process of choosing what you eat on a daily basis. The result will reenergize and revitalize your body. Your cravings will slowly disappear.

Make this promise to yourself right now: I will prioritize my recovering from Binge Eating Disorder. And I will keep that promise until food no longer controls me. From this point on, I control my food.

Repeat, and repeat, and repeat! This book will arm you with the tools you need to reach out for help and build your new life. So if you're ready, I am inviting you into a new world. Consider me in your corner for the long run. Now let's begin, together.

Wait! Before You Start...

I know you're anxious to get started, but before you do, I want to tell you about a free companion resource for this book.

As you'll find out in Chapter 4, keeping a journal is a great way to keep track of your progress and increase your awareness of the emotional triggers that lead to binge eating. But there's evidence that you can reduce the frequency and intensity of binges just by taking the time to track them!

In addition to journaling, I suggest you keep a separate record of your binge eating episodes. This is a space where you can record the times that you binge eat, what you ate, and how you felt afterward. I also recommend recording how hungry or full you felt immediately before and after the binge.

To make this easier for you, I've put together a worksheet with all the appropriate columns and a hunger scale that you can use to quickly rate your hunger before and after binges. You can download the worksheet for free at my website:

https://www.bcfpublishing.com/bingedownload

Simply print it out and keep it handy for your next binge. Even if you've sworn you'll never binge again, it's better to have it just in case. And don't beat yourself up when you do binge. You're only tracking to understand your behavior and triggers, not to punish yourself.

I know you're just starting your journey, but I don't want you to have to wait until Chapter 4 to get this benefit, so download the worksheet and get started today.

CHAPTER 1

Learning About Binge Eating Disorder

"NOTHING WILL WORK UNLESS YOU DO."
– MAYA ANGELOU

What is Binge Eating Disorder?

Most of us have had times when we've over-indulged in the foods we enjoy. Whether out of stress or for our own satisfaction, it's likely that we've all had overeating behaviors at some point in our lives. There are different levels of binge eating. But Binge Eating Disorder (BED) is defined by two main components: large amounts of food consumption, often at one time, and a pronounced feeling of loss of control. (If you find yourself overeating regularly, but not all at once, please do not feel excluded from the definition. The definition of BED includes you, too. The problem you are experiencing is just as valid as that of people who consume large amounts of food in one interval).

I want to share some good news with you: As of 2013, Binge Eating Disorder is included in the DSM-5 as an eating disorder diagnosis. (In case you're not familiar with it, the DSM is the Diagnostic and Statistical Manual of Mental Disorders, which is the research-based, official reference for mental health diagnoses). The book is essential because it basically makes sure that we're all on a similar page and speaking the same language when it comes to mental disorders.

The previous DSM, released in 1994, listed binge eating under the Eating Disorder Not Otherwise Specified category. Needless to say, this was a result and a perpetuation of the stigma and lack of understanding that surrounds the disorder. Today, some of that confusion has been cleared up. Over the last two decades, extensive research has shown the validity and consistency of this disorder.

In other words, Binge Eating Disorder is real, and if you suffer from it, there *is* help available. There are also many helpful, supportive communities in real time and online. There are safe spaces full of people who can relate to your experience. Good support groups encourage you to share only as much as you're comfortable with, but even just listening to others can be an asset to you on your journey. Hearing the stories of others will help you realize that you're not alone. But we will touch on that much more in depth later.

For now, let's get to know Binge Eating Disorder and its diagnostic features. Basically, we're going to go over the most important things to know about BED. First, it's recurrent. Episodes can have different triggers, or they can be induced by the same ones every time. In my case, stress, anxiety, and lack of self-care were major triggers. But people can overeat for different reasons, such as grief or depression. In any case, BED usually involves eating much more quickly than usual and eating beyond the point when one feels full. People who struggle with BED often eat until they experience physical discomfort and sometimes continue even after that. If you've ever eaten more than you can handle in one sitting, then you know what I mean. Your stomach hurts, you feel nauseated, and you can't imagine how you're going to lift yourself up from your chair.

With Binge Eating Disorder, the urge to continue eating feels so intense that it becomes a compulsion. It sometimes drives you even past the point of extreme discomfort. As we continue, you'll learn that this is partly because binge eating is a learned coping mechanism that we use when some other aspect of our lives has become too much or too painful to handle. In other words, we are numbing our emotions or trying to gain control over our situation or stress levels. But instead of addressing the problem, binge eating becomes a means of escape. The temporary relief it provides is never enough. That's partly because binge eating is a subconscious way of running away from problems, and the problems only get bigger when they're not dealt with them head-on. Food becomes a crutch rather than a means of nurturing yourself and maintaining homeostasis in the body.

Many times, people who suffer from BED eat alone, or at the very least overeat alone. This is because they are embarrassed and ashamed of how much they are eating. When binge eating was still a way of life for me, I carried a deep sense of shame that constantly ate away at me. I would go to any length to hide my problem from the people I lived and worked with. This is important: one of the hallmarks of BED is the feeling of shame and self-disgust that follows an overeating episode. No matter what the individual triggers are, BED is rooted in a state of mind when one has lost control over his or her life. If we can't control our lives, we try to control our food intake. In this way, it has a commonality with anorexia nervosa or bulimia nervosa, which have been much more recognized by the medical community. But Binge Eating Disorder is its own specific disorder with its own unique set of causes, symptoms, and behaviors. As such, it requires its own unique treatment.

Despite its historical lack of recognition by the medical community and society, BED is actually the most common disorder in the United States. Read that again. Binge Eating Disorder is *the most common eating disorder in the United States.*

Here are the facts: in adults, BED affects 3.5% of women and 2% of men. Interestingly, in women, it is most common in early adulthood. Yet it is more common in men as they reach middle age. Despite the cultural aspects that influence eating in general, BED does not seem to vary among races.

Binge Eating Disorder often has comorbid problems. This means that it can be accompanied by potentially severe physical and psychiatric issues or diagnoses. Most people with obesity don't also have BED, and making that association would be very wrong. But up to 2/3 of people with BED are obese, which can lead to a multitude of medical issues such as high blood pressure, diabetes, heart disease, stroke, cancer, osteoarthritis and breathing problems related to asthma or sleep apnea. Getting BED under control can transform your physical as well as your psychological health.

The Concept of Food Addiction

Although Binge Eating Disorder is finally receiving some critical recognition in the fields of psychiatry and psychology, the general concept of food addiction is still controversial. There is definitely a physiological component to food addiction. But even the medical field seems only to give it partial recognition. This is frustrating for people who struggle with BED, including myself, because years of scientific research shows that some foods are genuinely addictive.

Whether you become addicted or not depends on complex factors that vary from person to person. Binge Eating Disorder is complicated, but so are other addictions and psychological disorders. If you've been reading up to this point and feel you have a food addiction, the most crucial piece of advice I can give you is to *listen to your body and instincts.* Food addiction is very real. I'm here to provide you with the foundation of knowledge you need to understand how it is affecting you, and how to heal from it.

Evidence strongly suggests that certain foods, namely those high in sugar, may be capable of triggering an addictive response in prone individuals. Let's be real: to a degree, this describes all of us. Yet some of us are especially vulnerable to these addictive food characteristics. Along with many others who have BED, I struggled with reward dysfunction and impulsivity. Reward dysfunction describes both a psychological state and an actual chemical condition in the brain: the two are closely linked. Eating can be a powerful source of pleasure, and offering food as a reward can be an equally powerful motivation.

How many of us have heard as children, "If you eat all of the dinner on your plate, you can have extra dessert?" If you're like most people who were kids in the 80s and 90s, you heard a lot of, "If you're really good at school today, I promise to buy you a special treat." After all, food doesn't just meet energy needs and fuel the body systems to function. It also offers pleasure, and that pleasure is something you want to *hold onto* in your treatment.

We'll talk more later about the mistake of making food the enemy. We'll also talk more about the ways in which we can transform our attitude toward food, and the resulting love-hate relationship we have with it. For now, I want you to understand that food addiction occurs in the mind *and* the body. I don't want to bore you with too much science, but I feel it's vital to cover all areas that potentially contribute to Binge Eating Disorder.

If you're interested in learning more about the physiological factors that contribute to BED, here's a digestible fact: leptin is a protein produced by fat cells. Its primary function is to regulate appetite and fat storage. In people with congenital leptin deficiency, the sight of food increases activity in the dorsal and ventral striatum of the brain. These parts of the brain strongly influence brain reward circuits. Yet in people with leptin deficiency, leptin replacement therapy neutralizes both this brain activity and the intensity of food cravings. This is just one of the findings that support the idea that there's a physical element to overeating.

Studies have also shown a link between high-sugar diets to a deficit in the brain reward function. Very similar shortages in brain reward function have been reported in cocaine and heroin addiction. The suggestion here is that diet also influences brain cycles that could lead to overeating. Yet we don't ever want to cut the things we enjoy out of our diet completely. In fact, that's the opposite of what we want to do. Let me explain.

Why Traditional Dieting Never, Ever Works

Dieting is counterproductive to recovering from Binge Eating Disorder. Period. While it's necessary to establish healthy eating patterns in your daily life, the word "diet" has an undeniable stigma attached to it. Diets can seem like easy fixes because they eliminate food choices for you. If you're like I was, you may think, "If I follow a diet low in sugar and fat, I'll have no choice but to lose weight!" For a couple of days or even weeks, you're imbued with a renewed sense of purpose and accomplishment. ("Look at me, I lost three pounds! I knew I could do it if I just put my mind to it!") But actually, diets are usually only short-term solutions.

Listen closely: adopting a new eating pattern won't help heal the psychological and emotional problems that binge eating masks. But even when it comes to food itself, standard diets usually involve cutting out or heavily restricting the intake of certain foods. When you do this, you feel a sense of deprivation that only intensifies the cravings you're trying to escape by dieting.

Yet in our weight-obsessed culture, the media is flooded by diet culture, and our self-image is distorted by it. Everywhere we look, we are bombarded by ads featuring seemingly "perfect" women with unrealistic, airbrushed bodies. We are promised that we, too, can look that way if we just adopt this or that diet. Billions of dollars are spent on fad diet products each year, and social media has amplified the problem tenfold. Catchy digital effects are used to bring advertisements to life, making the desired effects all the more enviable. Social media influencers with millions of followers endorse diet products daily, dropping names of celebrities who "changed their lives" with everything from "fit tea" and plant-based diets to isogenics.

I want to be clear: diets that require intermittent periods of fasting, such as isogenics or various "juice fasts," are *not* healthy for people with Binge Eating Disorder and can even be dangerous. BED means that we struggle physically and emotionally with food addiction, and depriving ourselves only exacerbates the cycle of overeating. It also perpetuates the deeply ingrained, harmful belief that our desire for food is shameful and negative.

One of the most harmful misconceptions perpetuated by a toxic diet culture is that changing your eating habits leads to better self-esteem. Yes, unhealthy eating habits (including overeating and undereating disorders) are harmful to health, and the resulting physical and emotional problems reduce self-esteem. But changing your eating habits alone does not even begin to address the self-esteem problems that lead to disordered eating in the first place. In the same vein, dieting does not facilitate a healthier, more loving attitude toward food and your relationship with it. In order to rebuild your relationship with food and make it a healthy one, *you must have a healthy relationship with yourself.*

Losing weight may make you feel better about yourself in certain aspects. It certainly makes you feel better about yourself physically, at least for a while. And when you feel beautiful on the outside, it translates to the inside, right? Yet this is wrong. We've all been taught that much of our self-worth is determined by the way we look. (This is true for everyone in society, especially women). We live in a weight-obsessed culture where entire industries feed off our collective belief that we are not good enough the way we are.

But when it comes to dieting, if it seems too good to be true, it is. Believe me. Most diets result in a weight cycling effect that neither helps us lose weight or helps us form a more balanced relationship with food. You may not be ready to fully absorb this yet, but this type of unbalanced eating can harm our health and metabolism more than a little bit of extra weight *ever* will. In fact, restrictive fad diets almost always result in even further weight gain. More to the detriment of the people who use them, they can also be gateways to eating disorders.

That's right. Together we are breaking down the distortions about women's eating patterns that have become barriers. I am going to guide you through the process of developing an attitude about eating that supports a balanced diet you *enjoy* while restoring your health.

Our society's negative attitude toward food has made enjoying it a taboo, and that's wrong. These ideas are obstacles to developing healthy relationships with food and ourselves. I am here to help you overcome the cycle of negative self-talk, yo-yo dieting, and binging again. And I will be with you every step of the way.

CHAPTER 2

Committing to the Change

"Commitment means staying loyal to what you said you were going to do long after the mood you said it in has left you."

— Anonymous

Taking Control of Your Life Means Choosing Self-love, Everyday

Choose self-love. Everyday. Choosing self-love and adopting a kind attitude toward yourself is not optional. It's not a step you can skip over and still overcome low self-esteem, Binge Eating Disorder, and poor stress management. Skipping over this step is tempting for many, and you are not alone. For me, committing to making a change was daunting, but it wasn't the hardest part. After all, I am a strong woman who had committed to many things before. I was wholly committed to my job, my marriage, and doing it all.

So, after I committed to making a change and stumbled upon this hardest step of all, I had to ask myself why it was so difficult to relate to myself with kindness and empathy instead of self-loathing. I knew that my feelings of self-loathing were both triggered and perpetuated by binge eating. I always knew that if I wanted to make any real progress, my attitude toward myself had to shift from a place of self-hatred to self-love.

First of all, I believe that our culture teaches from a young age to value success over happiness, hard work over self-care. Like many other cultures of the world, we are defined as an independent culture as opposed to an interdependent one. Therein lays the internal conflict we face: every society is interconnected because human beings are interdependent by nature. This is true on an evolutionary level. It is biologically ingrained in us. So, any society that places most of its emphasis on the independent parts of human nature is creating an imbalance, an internal dysfunction we individually try to compensate for by scaling our perceived weaknesses like mountains.

We are taught to be inherently ashamed of our emotional responses to life events. Expressing profound sadness, processing grief at our own speed, and reaching out to others for help and support is not generally encouraged by any productivity-obsessed culture. Fortunately, this is changing. An emerging counterculture of people, comprised mainly of millennials and even younger groups, are advocating publicly for self-love and self-care. This movement of people is gaining momentum and stresses the importance of prioritizing wellness over productivity and setting your own standards for happiness.

Over the years, our society has sent us, to our detriment, a powerful message: Embracing our emotions and vulnerabilities is weak, and we can overcome these inherent weaknesses by working harder. Yet when we internalized this distorted values system, we end up skipping over the self-love stage of recovery. Take it from someone who's been there: skipping over this part just leads to more binge eating and more self-hatred. Self-berating and self-loathing is a trigger, and so are the feelings of hopelessness, depression, and low self-esteem that result from it.

So how did I break the cycle? Well, my self-love started as a learned behavior. A part of me wanted to heal and take control of my health and happiness so badly that I'd made the most difficult commitment of my life. That had to mean something, right? It meant that deep down, I loved myself. It also said that deep down, I had the desire to take a more holistic approach to healing: one that addressed my interconnected mind, body, and spirit. That desire had taken root and wanted to grow into something beautiful, but I had to take the first step. That first step was to treat myself kindly when the urge to overeat overcome me physically, mentally, and emotionally.

I won't lie to you; it overcame me many times, which I learned was normal as I got further into the healing process. Sometimes, I would feel so disgusted with myself for being overtaken by stress that I raged inside, heading straight toward the refrigerator to escape from my intense feelings of self-loathing. In those moments, I absolutely hated myself for what I perceived as my weakness. Well, we all have our Achilles' heel to contend with, don't we? I would reason with myself, rationalizing the temptation to overeat. But then something turned me around.

What marked my second step toward recovery from BED was this: I asked myself what "weaknesses" were fueling such intense self-hatred, driving me toward the fridge for salvation. In other words, I posed variations of this same question to myself: Lauren, what's making you so upset that you believe binge eating is your only escape? What feelings are you experiencing inside that are too uncomfortable to sit with, to feel? Then, even though I didn't feel it yet, I practiced self-love. I walked away from the fridge *before* binge eating and addressed myself with love.

Because visuals make solid impressions, I sometimes actually looked in the mirror as I spoke to myself kindly. In my head or aloud, I said to myself, "I am so proud of myself for resisting temptation tonight." I was feeling so lonely, and that's a painful way to feel. Yet I was able to sit with the feeling without numbing it over by overeating. That's a wonderful accomplishment. On the rare occasions that I binged, I was able to stop myself. When I did, I stopped beating myself up with the old familiar, chastening belt. I told myself, "It's okay to make mistakes. I forgive you, and we will do better tomorrow. It's going to be okay."

The Evolutionary Case for Interdependent Support Systems

The need for social interaction and belonging is part of human nature and has been historically evidenced over time. Some scientific theories strongly suggest that during the earliest stage of humanity, humans became collaborative foragers for survival. What does this mean? Well, it means that humans met their survival needs by living and working with each other to find and share food and shelter. They became interdependent in the most basic way. They benefited from the well-being other the people with whom they spent their time. Humans began to evolve partly by learning new skills for collaboration. In this vein, entire complex cultures were formed and continued to grow. We are still evolving every day.

The point of sharing this is not to give you a history lesson. It's to help you understand that your need for a support system, a shoulder to cry on, is within your human nature.

Shifting From A Place of Self-Loathing to Self-Love: A Learned Behavior

Within my so-called "weakness" lies my emotional core. I am a caring, highly sensitive person with an endless depth of love inside. I deserve the freedom to share myself with the world, and so do you.

Ever so slowly, I realized that kind self-talk was beginning to come more naturally than self-berating! I couldn't believe it. I was actually internalizing the self-loving behaviors that I'd taught myself. Before that point in time, I had had fleeting moments of self-love, contentment, and even joy and ecstasy. I had found the love of my life and married him; we had recently moved into a new condo that I adored, and I was living out my years with my favorite person in the world. These were things to celebrate, and I did. But I never had enough inner happiness to sustain this state of joy and gratitude. Now that I was starting to love myself, I had so much more to give to my husband, my home, and my work. I was actually more productive than I had been when I was pushing myself to the point of neglecting self-care- and binge eating as a result.

I don't mean to sound redundant, but I really can't emphasize enough the harmful effects of living in a society in which success is prioritized over happiness. Negative self-talk is disguised as motivation: everywhere you look on TV, social media, or in magazines, some influencer is proclaiming their victory over food. Yet food is not the enemy. Negative self-talk is! I promise you that any so-called motivational influencer who promotes fad diets and correlates positive self-esteem with weight loss is not a health advocate. Sure, losing weight makes you feel good about yourself when you are overweight. It should. It means you're physically moving in a healthy direction. It can also mean that you've improved your eating habits, which is no small feat and a cause for pride! The danger is in taking care of your body while ignoring your emotional and psychological health.

The danger is in perceiving your natural, human needs and vulnerabilities as weaknesses. This often leads to the belief that squashing your weaknesses like a bug is the right path to strength, which is a delusion. You've got to get to know the needs, emotions, and vulnerabilities that caused you to start binge eating in the first place. You've got to get to know your inner self, relate to that hidden person with kindness, and learn how to love him or her. Learn how to meet her needs and get her needs met by others.

A small percentage of society is nurtured adequately as children and taught to love themselves exactly as they are. But usually, those not taught how to love themselves have great difficulty teaching their children how to do just that. Women who were taught that being thin means being beautiful, and being beautiful is the only means of female power, teach their children the same thing. Men who were trained that masculinity means suppressing emotions teach their sons to hide theirs, too. Binge eating is just one manifestation of repressed feelings, pain, or trauma. Some people, including those who suffer from anorexia or bulimia nervosa, use deprivation to control their lives and emotions.

It may sound like a tired cliché, but loving your inner child the way he or she deserves to be loved is worth your time. It's also the most integral step to changing your relationship with food after you've been diagnosed with Binge Eating Disorder.

Repeat positive affirmations in your head: I am beautiful the way I am. I am powerful and capable of changing my eating habits and creating a healthier me. I am worthy of happiness and health. It's okay to put myself first, and I am proud of myself for doing so when I have been taught not to.

Sometimes there's no getting over a problem; you've got to go through it and give yourself as long as it takes. Sometimes food cushioned me when I felt insecure; it provided me with the insulation I needed when I wasn't feeling safe from the situations in my life. Other times, I had tried to fill my loneliness with food. I was so used to holding everything in to maintain a picture-perfect image that I had stopped sharing with the people I loved, including my husband.

That realization made me so sad that I thought of drowning my sorrow in excess, in pasta, in ice cream. But I knew that I would never form new, healthier habits if I didn't consciously replace the old with the new. How would I ever get my needs met if I didn't reach out to my husband, friends, and family? It wasn't easy, but I gradually accepted my dependency needs and learned how to ask for help and support when I most needed it. As a result, some meaningful relationships in my life experienced a transformation that I never thought possible.

Now, I want to take a moment to talk to you about a potentially painful part of the recovery process. You are intrinsically connected to the networks of people in your lives, including family, friends, and co-workers. Thus, changes you make affect people around you, and the changes they make also affect you. It's inevitable. But there's a high likelihood that some people in your life have not begun to recover from the illnesses or negative patterns that brought them down. They may have emotional reactions to the positive changes you are making, and may not even know how to identify or process these feelings. Many people are mired in low self-esteem and existing in a way that has more to do with responsibility than joy. Like I once was, some of my friends were running on empty as I was starting my healing journey; some were unhappy with their lot in lives and convinced there was nothing they could do to change it.

Some of these people showed abject cynicism toward my newfound self-love and my belief in the power to change my own life. I started making time to indulge in hobbies I loved even though they brought in no money and, thus, were deemed silly dalliances by a few people I truly loved and valued. My mother worried that the few hours of overtime I gave up would break my bank and put my husband and me in debt. At first, my husband did, too. But I made it clear to him how important it was for me to carve out time for the artistic endeavors I had long abandoned. When he realized how much it meant to me, we reasonably discussed our budget and decided that the overtime wasn't going to make or break us. He agreed that if I didn't have an outlet for self-expression outside our marriage and my work, I was more likely to turn to binge eating to fulfill that need.

That, in essence, is what I am trying to convey to you: the people who are truly healthy additions to your life, and are genuinely committed to their relationship with you, will support your needs. Although differences may arise, they will work through them with you.

Notice that I didn't say, "The people who truly love you will stay by your side and support the healthy changes you are making." I didn't say it because it's not necessarily true. Some people really do love and care about you, but they're not in the right emotional place to be a supportive influence in your life. There are certainly toxic influences that feed off of your un-happiness and discard you when they can no longer manipulate or put you down. There are also people who are codependent on you and react with volatility or distancing when you set much-needed boundaries. But not everyone falls into these categories. Sadly, sometimes, people are just on different levels of heal-ing, focused on different things, and grow apart.

If you find yourself losing loved ones when you make progress, don't try to repress your grief. This can be a profoundly sad experience that shakes your world, contributes to a sense of instability or even results in major depression. This is especially true when the loss is an intimate partner, close friend, or beloved family member. If you stumble upon this kind of crisis or difficulty on your recovery journey, I strongly encourage you to seek the support of a ther-apist well-versed in eating disorders. It doesn't have to be a roadblock, but it can be a painful trigger that intensifies the urge to overeat.

I was never a fan of the old adage, "You're born alone, and you die alone, so you might as well get used to it." (I forget exactly how it goes, and the In-ternet has undoubtedly produced massive variations of it, but it goes something like that). Although there is some truth to the idea that life is essentially your own journey, and it can be a lonely one at times, I've adopted a more positive outlook on the human con-dition. The fact that we are all interconnected can be

COMMITTING TO THE CHANGE

a highly rewarding aspect of human nature. But it can also inevitably be painful, such as during the loss of a relationship or a loved one either through death or separation. At these times, it's important to remember that a great deal of happiness comes from within. Positive, meaningful relationships serve to enhance this happiness and definitely become part of it. But they do not create it on their own, and even after a profound loss, there is a reason to go forward. That reason is you.

Defining Self-love and Happiness: Only You Know What It Looks Like For You

Happiness is not a textbook definition, and neither is self-love. Ideally, growth should be celebrated more than achievement. This is because our achievements, although important, represent only a part of our experience. Have you ever met someone with a great career, but a floundering personal life? I've known my share of successful, self-motivated women who are nonetheless living in continual personal distress. Many come from families with extremely unhealthy beauty standards that they've projected onto us. Even if you're among the lucky few whose family encourages you to celebrate and love yourself exactly as you are, you may have internalized societal pressures on women. (I think to a degree, we all have. It's just a matter of how well you transcend these distortions).

Because society focuses more on external achievements than internal growth, or achievements that happen outside of a preconceived box of expectations, we often do the same: we measure ourselves based on what we've accomplished on paper. We measure our worth by our looks and productivity. The problem with this is that it means our focus is on living a life that makes others happy or keeps up with societal standards for success. Many times, the things we are focusing on go against the grain of our true desires. The result is a yawning chasm between who we are and who we want to be, a misalignment that creates all sorts of physical and mental imbalances. Trust me, once this disparity sets in, it affects all aspects of our well-being. I used to get stuck thinking, *Maybe I shouldn't be prioritizing my relationship and self-care right now. I was so naïve, thinking I could have it all.* But I was wrong. I could have it all, within reason.

You are challenged to define what happiness and success mean to you, and live accordingly. I know it's not easy. Let's say, for example, you hate your job. It monopolizes all your time, doesn't ignite your passion and leaves little time and energy for the activities that bring you joy. You keep working harder and harder, but you're beginning to feel exhausted and dead inside. Depression sets in, and then you start to notice physical manifestations of your distress. I'm asking you to view these physical signs as your body's way of telling your mind that it's time to make a change.

Maybe you can't change everything all at once, and that's okay. Changing your career, or even making shifts within your career, is not an overnight process. But deciding to make the changes, writing down a clear set of goals regarding those changes, and taking small steps toward them gives you a sense of control.

The Role of Neuroplasticity in Everyday Life

Now we're going to define neuroplasticity and talk about how you can use it to augment the healing process. Neuroplasticity is a term that refers to the physiological changes that occur in the brain in response to our environment. In other words, when we interact with others and our environment, our brains make new connections between neurons. It's something that happens naturally, but we can encourage and stimulate the process. This way, we're training our brains to help us adjust and accommodate to our ever-shifting needs.

Adapting a growth mindset enhances the positive effects of neuroplasticity. What is a growth mindset? Well, it's essentially defined as the belief that one's skills, talents, and abilities can be developed and/or improved with determination. Neuroplasticity, which describes the brain's ability to adapt and develop based on our changing circumstances as adults, is triggered by a growth mindset. This connection is important because it tells us that, to a degree, we can change our brain chemistry by changing our own mindset! Because the brain is the control center of the body, it also means we can change the way our body systems function.

We know that chronic, long-term exposure to stress depletes the cortisol levels that help regulate the immune system and inflammation levels in the body. During acute stress, cortisol levels increase during the fight or flight response, which gives the body enough energy to cope with a real or perceived threat. How does cortisol provide us with this energy? It metabolizes glucose and fatty acids from the liver. This is an ingrained, life-saving mechanism. When we experience prolonged, repeated exposure to acute stress, our cortisol supply decreases. Increased heart rate and other autonomic reactions result in severe wear and tear on the body systems. Chronic stress predisposes the human body to metabolic imbalances and a host of diseases and disorders. These include heart disease, immune suppression and autoimmunity, gastrointestinal disorders, and countless other problems. Many of these can become debilitating and life-threatening over time.

Now, add binge eating to this cycle, and many imbalances caused by stress are exacerbated. Some people with BED do maintain a normal weight, which presents yet another challenge: the fear that they won't be taken seriously when they seek help for the disorder. Many individuals with BED do become overweight or obese. This can result in cardiovascular disease, high cholesterol and blood pressure, and the onset of diabetes. When the cardiovascular, circulatory and metabolic systems are already taxed by chronic stress, the physical taxation of obesity is often the proverbial "straw that breaks the camel's back." In other words, a heart attack, diabetes diagnosis, or other serious health problem can be the breaking point that signifies a need for help and treatment for BED.

Psychologically, we've got to break the barriers that stop us from addressing BED and seek help from our support systems and medical professionals. One of these barriers is weight stigma. Because being overweight is so looked down on in society, people who suffer from BED can be paralyzed with the fear of admitting they have this problem. Being overweight is too often associated with undesirable character traits such as laziness, gluttony, or irresponsibility.

But this is not reality; it's a method of fat-shaming that feeds a consumer-oriented society in which men and women spend billions of dollars per day on fad diets and weight loss products or programs that guarantee instant gratification. Both being overweight and suffering from binge eating disorder, which can be mutually exclusive, are real medical problems with physiological factors. Overweight people are not necessarily this way because of psychological issues; many suffer from metabolic imbalances such as polycystic ovary disorder or hypothyroidism that make it very difficult to maintain a healthy weight. In the same vein, not everyone who has binge eating disorder is overweight.

Normalizing a binge eating disorder and getting society to recognize it as a real disorder is critically important. Many people are starting to realize it and are engaging in a worldwide conversation about it. But first, you have to heal yourself. Society does not define your happiness or your ideal weight: you do. You may be surprised to learn that BMI charts and medical weight standards determined by the CDC only give us ranges of ideal weights for our height. They don't take into account body structure, bone density, or each person's unique metabolic composition, including blood pressure, cholesterol levels, genetics, and much more. There are ranges for healthy weights. Only you, the right medical professional, and possibly a mental health provider get to decide what you should weigh.

Healing starts from within, not with a number. There is no easy, trending fix for Binge Eating Disorder, but there is an abundance of help and support available. As someone who struggled with Binge Eating Disorder for years and overcame it, I'm here to help you begin.

CHAPTER 3

The Road to Recovery

"Sometimes you can only find Heaven by slowly backing away from Hell."

– Carrie Fisher

Identifying Your Triggers

This section will focus on the positive parts of the journey to recovery from Binge Eating Disorder. But before you can get to the point when recovery becomes exciting, you need to identify your triggers. Sometimes, you need the help of a counselor or therapist to do this, and that's okay. If you've realized that your thoughts shift to food whenever you have an emotion or situation you want to avoid, you've come a long way already. Now you just have to identify what those feelings and situations are.

Like in many families, mine was not very comfortable with talking about feelings. I internalized those habits along with the belief that there is something shameful about letting outsiders know you are vulnerable on the inside. But the fact is, everyone is vulnerable on the inside. Our parents grew up in a repressive culture, and although a major shift is happening regarding our generation's attitude toward sharing and vulnerability, our generation is still repressive in many ways. We're too focused on external markers of success: many times, we're busy, successful people balancing too much, and we've got no outlet when we feel stressed. In part, because we haven't been taught how to talk about or relate to our feelings, and, thus, we don't know how to reach out for help. Most of us also haven't been taught how to self-soothe; instead, we grew up looking to outside sources for pleasure, comfort, and validation. I know this was true for me. If it's true for you, too, then it's time to start getting to know yourself.

Getting to know yourself means delving deep into experiences, feelings, and beliefs about yourself that you may have repressed. While this can be scary and require you to reach out for help from a counselor, therapist, or eating disorder specialist, it can also be the most exciting thing you've ever done. At the beginning of my journey, I really did hate myself in many ways. I would never in a million years have dreamt that any part of getting to know myself inside could bring me joy. But once I made peace with the things about myself I used to judge and shame, I unlocked even deeper, more beautiful sides of myself.

Sides I was too afraid to know before because they made me inherently vulnerable. Sharing myself so deeply added a new depth and dimension of intimacy to the important relationships in my life.

So, let's talk about your triggers. Were you raised in a repressive or restrictive environment in which you couldn't express your feelings comfortably? Take a moment to imagine yourself as the child you once were. Now, if you can, embody this child. If it's possible, don't just think about this exercise. Let go of the present moment, open up, and go back to one of the most painful moments you experienced as a child. (If you can't emotionally connect to the memory, that's okay, too. Go back there with your mind and do this brief exercise on an intellectual level; there is something valuable to be learned from it). When you've come up with a memory, recall the details. How did you feel? What was upsetting to you? Where were you at that moment? Was it your living room or elementary school? Whatever the situation was, use your sense memory to call up the details so that it may begin to feel as if you're actually there.

Once you've remembered how you felt and why you felt that way, ask yourself this: Was anyone there to comfort you? If they were, did you feel safe, understood, and loved? If the answers to these questions are "no," then you might have discovered one reason you rely on food for comfort as an adult.

If you came from an open, supportive family, take a look at other places, you might have learned to suppress your feelings and vulnerabilities. The school years alone can be enough to cause long-term damage to many of us. If you were bullied or picked on as a child or a teen, you might have hidden yourself away from your peers and turned to food for comfort. Much of our self-image and self-esteem is shaped by our relationships with peers at school. Even popular kids usually had to play a role and conceal what they felt would be perceived as weaknesses from others.

Too often, there is a "survival of the fittest" mentality accompanying the elementary and high school experience. To stay at the top of the food chain, you've got to pick on those at the bottom. If you found yourself at the bottom, the damage to your self-esteem might have been serious and long-lasting. If you were lost somewhere in the middle, you might have felt as if you didn't truly belong anywhere. The list of problems could go on and on. The purpose of this reflection is to identify the point in time when you first learned to repress your feelings and turned to food for comfort.

I know I mentioned this in some detail earlier in this book, but it's worth emphasizing that if you've experienced trauma, neglect or abuse, it's a good idea to work toward recovery with the help and support of a professional. Identifying your binge eating triggers will eventually bring out the memory of your trauma, and you may feel as if you're living it all over again. This kind of experience is extremely intense and painful, so my advice is that you do this with a professional who can provide the support you need. If you enter into those memories before you are ready or without a professional support system, there is the potential to resort to binge eating or even more destructive behaviors. There's also the potential to experience an emotional or psychological crisis or breakdown, which is nothing to be ashamed of. It just requires the knowledge and help of someone who is trained to work with people who've experienced serious trauma. If you're one of the many people who need to recover from a traumatic childhood or a traumatic event that occurred at any age, I am here for you. This book is for you, too.

Consider the relationship between a parent and a child. Ideally, that bond is marked by a strong element of symbiosis, and the child's physical and emotional needs are fulfilled. If this was not the case, the child naturally feels as if something essential is missing inside. In a sense, it is; the nurturing aspect between parent and child aids physiologically and psychologically in development. So, he or she does not learn at that essential early age how to get dependency needs met. There are many potential manifestations of an absent or abusive early relationship with caregivers. One of the ways in which children who have not been comforted learn to comfort themselves is Binge Eating Disorder.

It should also be noted that much of our relationship with food was learned from the childhood environment. Ask yourself: did your parents or caregivers have a healthy relationship with food? Many people with BED grew up in environments in which others overate to deal with difficult emotions and situations. Others with BED faced the opposite challenge: One or more key figures in their childhood had restrictive attitudes toward food, placed an unhealthy emphasis on staying thin, or measured their worth based on appearance. Although not always, this type of environment is often fraught with the pressure to succeed academically and/or socially at all costs —even at the expense of your health.

Remember, parents who have not resolved certain issues within themselves often unconsciously pass those same issues onto their children. (It's like an enormous inheritance, only instead of unlimited shopping sprees, it's lots of pain and psychological resonance). The point of acknowledging this fact is that it illuminates an important cornerstone of your recovery journey: *Just because your parents or caregivers had an unhealthy relationship with themselves or with food, doesn't mean you have to.* There is so much power in this statement. You have within you the power to heal your relationship with yourself and change your relationship with food from toxic to healthy and delicious.

That's right. Recovery from binge eating disorder is not about dietary restrictions. It's about learning to eat intuitively and listen to your body. It is this premise upon which you will learn to make healthier choices and build a beneficial, *pleasurable* relationship with food. Because contrary to what fad diet campaigns would have you believe, your guilt cannot be assuaged by adhering to a certain diet. It can only be healed by changing how you relate to food and yourself. There is a highly synergistic relationship between eating and emotions. Mine used to be highly disordered and deeply in conflict. It is now harmonious and aligned for the most part. The best part of it is that food is still a source of comfort. It's just not the only source, and the comforting aspect is that I'm giving my body exactly what it needs.

We've discussed a variety of common triggers for binge eating, but everyone's individual triggers are unique. Only you can find the feelings you are avoiding when you overeat and process them. Yet it's important to not only have an emotional understanding of these issues but apply this understanding to your food choices. What do I mean by this? Well, let's talk about it.

I want you to be specific about your triggers in relation to food. If, for example, you often overeat on your lunch break at work, determine why this pattern began. What is the trigger? Let's say your work environment makes you feel inadequate, and the stress and pain of it triggers the need to overeat. If this is the case, find a private place to write or type the following sentence: *When I feel inadequate at work, I feel triggered to binge eat.* It may sound overly simplistic, but I can't emphasize the importance of putting your triggers in a tangible, written form.

Once you've completed this step, remember that most triggers take time to resolve, so we've got to develop healthy coping mechanisms to deal with them while they exist. Staying with this example, what can you do to relieve your stress or comfort yourself when you feel inadequate at work? Write this down: When I feel inadequate at work, I have other options aside from binge eating. *I can vent to a friend. I can pull out my cell phone and scribble down my stress in the notes section. I can call my husband.* The key is that you have both short-term and long-term coping mechanisms that provide stress relief and comfort.

Don't underestimate the power of positive affirmations. One way to develop a strong, reliable relationship with yourself is to identify a list of positive beliefs about yourself and about your life. They can be simple and meditative, such as, *I am safe*, or *I am loved.* Affirmations like these send the brain the message that you are indeed safe. As the central organ in the body from which all others receive messages about how to function, the brain releases chemicals in response to our thoughts. When you tell yourself positive things, the brain releases endorphins that make you feel good and enhance the cellular processes that work to keep your body systems functioning optimally. Positive affirmations can stop the "fight or flight" stress response in its tracks. Remember that "fight or flight" is stimulated by perceived danger.

Once triggered, all of the body systems not required to maintain homeostasis under acute stress begin to shut down. This happens so that the systems needed to deal with acute stress have the energy to push forward. Thus, the central and autonomic nervous systems go into overdrive, releasing cortisol and raising your heart and blood pressure. Needless to say, the heart and circulatory system as a whole take a beating under chronic stress. Essentially, so do the systems that must be suppressed in order for the "fight or flight" response to thrive. This includes the immune system, which is one of the reasons you hear people say, "Stress makes you sick."

Positive affirmations can stop this stress response in its tracks and create a physiological process that is much healthier for you. My advice is to base positive affirmations on the things that trigger your negative feelings. Two types of affirmations worked best for me: affirmations that replaced my negative, limiting beliefs with positive ones and affirmations that offset negative beliefs and situations. For example, if my stress was situational, I used to find myself thinking, "My schedule is overflowing; there is no way

I'm going to be able to handle all of this! I'm so tired, I'm going to collapse!"

Now, I replace overwhelming, catastrophic thoughts like these with a more positive belief: "I have all the tools I need to manage my time and include self-care in my routine when my busy schedule gets overwhelming." In this vein, I am not denying that my current situation is stressful. I am fully acknowledging it. But I'm also consciously acknowledging that I have the tools I need to cope in the healthiest way possible with the situation at hand.

When a negative self-belief surfaces, I replace it with a positive one when I can. For example, sometimes, I find myself feeling weak when my body sends out signals of stress and exhaustion. It doesn't happen nearly as often as it used to, but there are times when I find myself thinking, "I'm not half as efficient as my co-workers. If I can't meet my deadlines, am I really all that valuable to my job?" Then I take a conscious step back and evaluate the reality of the situation, which is that I have many strengths that make me an invaluable asset to my job. The truth is that deadlines stress me the hell out, and I'm no longer ashamed to admit it to myself; everyone has strengths and weaknesses. Now I say to myself, "The work I produce is high quality and efficient, and I'm damn proud of it." That alone takes my stress down several notches, and the compulsory need to binge eat is much more manageable when it comes on.

Get Excited about Recovering from Binge Eating Disorder!

Yes, you heard me, right! (And no, I'm not clinically insane. I promise). One of the most important aspects of my recovery was my positive attitude about it. Just to be clear, that doesn't mean there weren't days when I felt so depressed and out of control that I was seconds away from binge eating. That's far from the truth! One of the main purposes of this book is for me to share my raw, honest experience with you so that you have a realistic idea of what the road to BED recovery really looks like, and so you don't feel alone. Yes, I absolutely did have days when I couldn't see my life through a positive lens, and I just had to muddle through until I had the physical and emotional energy to begin a new day with a new attitude. The point is, I never gave up. Now that I can honestly say I've made a full recovery, even the lowest lows were worth it.

Later in this book, I will guide you through the process of building a system of stress management strategies to rely on when the temptation to overeat is overwhelming. But for now, let's talk about food.

CHAPTER 4

Tracking Your Recovery

"I avoid looking forward or backward, and try to keep looking upward."

– Charlotte Brontë

Replacing the Diet Mentality with Intuitive Eating

Now that we've rejected the diet mentality let's replace it with something that feels and tastes much better. Start here: when you're hungry, honor that feeling. Hunger is the body's biologically ingrained way of letting us know it needs energy; that is something to celebrate, not reject.

Intuitive eating transcends the diet mentality by teaching us to listen to our bodies, not outside expectations. With intuitive eating, there is no counting calories or even following a meal plan. You may wonder how you could possibly get your excessive eating habits and consumption of sweets or other unhealthy foods under control without a strict diet plan. In fact, you may believe that your tendency toward binge eating means you need an even stricter, more regimented plan than the average person. But not only are diets harmful to people with BED (and other disorders such as anorexia and bulimia nervosa), you don't need them.

Why? The answer is simple: Your body has an ingrained sensor for what it needs to function optimally at any given moment. Intuitive eating puts you in tune with that internal sensor by transferring your focus to internal cues rather than external rules. Hunger, fullness, and satisfaction are all examples of internal cues that essentially let you know how much and what to eat. If you're lacking strength, feeling tired or sense the warning signs of a cold coming on, you may need to increase your protein and antioxidant intake. However, if you're feeling a bit shaky in the moment, you may need sugar or carbohydrates to raise your blood sugar, and that's okay, too. One of the premises of intuitive eating maintains that no foods are "bad foods" or "off limits." When you listen to the internal signals your body is sending you about food, you'll naturally avoid overconsumption of substances like sugar, saturated fats, bread, and white flour. You'll also avoid overeating. This is because your body will tell you when you're full and physically satisfied, cueing you to stop eating. Moderation comes to you naturally when you're eating intuitively.

In order to adopt intuitive eating in your life, first, you've got to make peace with food. You've been trained to believe that fattening or sugary foods are "bad," but this isn't true. Really, it isn't. Keep listening. Your body needs a certain amount of carbohydrates, which are converted to both sugars and energy. There is a use for sugar in the human diet. What you don't want is too much, but that does not mean it should be off limits. By labeling certain foods as taboo and relegating them to a list of guilty pleasures, guess what you're doing? You're intensifying your cravings. Deprivation always leads to craving, and no balance can be gleaned from that cycle. In fact, fad diet campaigns feed off of it, catching you in midswing between "good eating" and "bad eating" —and promising an easy fix to binge eating that doesn't exist. There's a reason why they say forbidden fruit always tastes better. In our minds, it does! That's why it's so imperative that you let go of this mentality and welcome all foods.

Psychologically, if you tell yourself that a certain food group you enjoy is "bad," you will eventually feel deprived. Feeling deprived naturally translates into intense cravings that are very difficult to control. You may resist the urge once, twice, or even for a certain tenuous amount of time. But the stress of balancing that tightrope between staying away and giving in leads to stress. As tension builds up, the desire to relieve the pressure becomes very real, and the temptation to overeat grows. That's why when you finally do give into the food you're craving, you tend to overeat. You're compensating for what your body and mind experienced as deprivation, and there's no real physiological need for this. More to the point, overeating triggers guilt; and guilt starts the cycle of deprivation, cravings, and overeating all over again.

Satisfaction plays a prominent role in eating, as it absolutely should. When you're feeling physically full yet unsatisfied by what you ate, it leaves you wanting more. That's why incorporating all of the foods you love into your diet actually helps you avoid overconsumption of less healthy food groups. Just like your body knows when it has had its fill of healthier foods, it knows when sweeter or more fattening tastes have been satiated. Know that this type of intuitive eating helps, but it does not always eliminate cravings. There is also the emotional side, and the emotional healing process is not an overnight journey. My advice is to be patient and compassionate with yourself throughout the process. After all, you are transforming your relationship with food *and* with yourself, which is incredibly brave. It's also the healthiest thing you can do for your body, much healthier than giving into the fad diets that cycle through an industry that profits from the toxic relationship with food it perpetuates.

You Are Not What You Eat

We've all heard the saying, *You are what you eat.* But I'm here to tell you that it isn't true. Yes, your food intake determines a lot about your health. But your worth is not a measure of how much or how little you eat. It is not measured by what you eat. Your worth has nothing at all to do with food. The association is a learned one that was introduced to you by society at a young age and is perpetuated by society throughout adult life. The only relationship between food and self-esteem lies in the false belief that your value is determined by what you eat and how you look. If you overeat or eat large amounts of unhealthy food at a time, you are still just as worthy. You will just be healthier physically and mentally if you learn to eat intuitive, which means incorporating many healthy foods that enhance rather than deplete your energy systems. But you're including these foods in your diet because your body needs and wants them, not be-cause you will look better or be a better person as a result.

This is a concept that often surfaces in anti-diet culture. It is sometimes referred to as "radical self-acceptance" by psychologists and leaders in the body positivity movement, but the implication is not that it is radical to love yourself the way you are, and sepa-rate food from self-worth. The inferred meaning of the term "radical self-acceptance" or "radical self-love" is that this mentality is only considered radical in a society that already has distorted constructs about food and self-worth. For me, internalizing this concept of "radical self-acceptance" meant that I had made a commitment to love myself no matter what stage I was in my relationship with food. It becomes an integral part of recovery because we have to be able to forgive ourselves if we do give in to the urge to overeat.

If you've given in to the urge to binge eat, forgive yourself. Tomorrow is a new day, and you can start again. The important thing is not to give into guilt and allow it to cause you such distress that you overeat again and again. If you've just given into temptation, replace your critical or self-loathing thoughts with positive ones. Tell yourself that you are human, and everyone on a recovery journey makes mistakes. Tell yourself that you are strong and capable of managing your stress without binge eating the next time. And then let it go.

When learning to rely on intuitive eating rather than dieting, ask yourself how you feel during and after the consumption of certain foods. Ask yourself how certain foods affect your mood. Tune into the taste, and even the texture of the food you are eating; pay attention to the way different parts of your body respond during and after eating. Contrary to what the competitive dieting industry proclaims in bold letters on billboards (and social media), there is no "one size fits all" when it comes to food choices. Some people feel energized by a diet high in meat-based proteins, and others have sensitive guts and difficulty processing large amounts of these foods. Yet others feel better when they get their protein from a vegan or vegetarian-based diet rich in nuts, beans, and a variety of delicious fruits and vegetables. When you tune into the way different foods make you feel, you're letting your body tell you what it needs, which is the best indicator of all.

If you overeat, use it as a window of opportunity to learn more about yourself and your body. How does your body feel during and after binge eating? What is it trying to tell you? Tuning into your body after binge eating and remembering how you felt while you were doing it can provide invaluable insights. This is because your body and mind are engaged in constant, fluid communication. Your body doesn't just have responses to the food you eat, but to the emotions, you feel while eating. These emotions, in turn, influence the body's metabolizing process, which directly affects how much nutrition you get from food. So, pay attention to your physical response to emotional stress, and how it influences your eating.

Pay attention to the physical sensations associated with cravings; they could be closely linked to the emotions you're trying to escape via the binge eating cycle. Also, absorb the way your body feels when the food is going down. Even the healthiest, most nutritious meals won't feel good in your stomach; the digestion process will be impaired, potentially causing pain or discomfort. Furthermore, the feeling of dissatisfaction will remain because binge eating is only a temporary balm for the underlying emotional causes of the disorder.

Now that you have an understanding of intuitive eating let's work on using it to change your behaviors and make different food choices.

Planning and Tracking Your Recovery: Journaling

When tracking your recovery, it can be extremely helpful to put your progress in writing. Journaling played a major role in my recovery because it not only helped me track my progress, but it also helped me identify some of my biggest triggers for binge eating. In the early stages of my recovery, I still had a lot of trouble talking about my struggle with Binge Eating Disorder and the pain it caused me. As I gradually got involved in cognitive behavioral therapy and learned new communication skills, I was eventually able to open up to my loved ones about it. But in the beginning, I didn't share my problem or the pain it had caused with anyone in my life. My journal became my best friend in recovery. And even though I'm now much better able to open up about my feelings and communicate effectively with the people I love, my journal is still a lifesaver.

I want you to purchase a journal. If you're already a journal keeper, buy a new one now, even if it's just a notebook from a convenience store that you pick up on your errands. Either buy a journal with a lock or, if it's a notebook or an open book, keep it tucked away somewhere only you have access to it. The point is that your writing stays private, and the writing is uninfluenced by anyone, but you as you record your thoughts, feelings, and behaviors. I don't mean to make it sound so formal, because the approach I recommend is actually the opposite. When you write in this journal for the first time, I want you to be spontaneous. Your entry doesn't have to seem like it has anything to do with Binge Eating Disorder. Just write about what you're feeling in the moment, and try not to filter your words through your thoughts. What I mean by this is, just write the words as they come and don't think about them. Don't worry about how they sound or make any judgments. It doesn't matter if your writing is an accurate account of actual events. The important thing is what you're feeling right now.

Write it down when you binge eat. This, of course, is not a way of punishing yourself. Instead, it's a way to gain insight about your triggers and make connections between your emotions and binge eating. Patterns will start to emerge with time, and your biggest triggers will become more obvious to you. Were the days or even hours before you overate filled with stress, extremely busy or overwhelming? How were you feeling inside? Many of us are triggered by certain emotions, such as loneliness, grief, or anger.

Anger, in particular, is an emotion that really seems to scare us, especially women. Traditionally, women were taught that aggression was unfeminine or showed a lack of manners and refinement, even when the anger was an appropriate response to a situation. Although society is becoming more progressive, there is still a long way to go, and as women, we tend to internalize this repressive mentality. This is especially true when we grew up in repressive households or were continually made to feel ashamed or embarrassed when we showed emotions.

There can also be cultural factors, as some cultures, societies, and religions are less expressive and interdependent than others. Men deal with their own cultural barriers when it comes to expressing vulnerability. Although to a degree, it's much more socially acceptable for men to show anger than women, men are often shamed or labeled weak for showing vulnerability. Crying has been taboo for men in most cultures for a long time, and as a society, we are only at the tip of the iceberg when it comes to an understanding of how distorted that double standard really is.

Anger is especially damaging when it becomes a roadblock to assertiveness. Being assertive means directly expressing your thoughts, beliefs, and wishes. In a conflict, assertive people aren't afraid to disagree with others, but they do so in a respectful rather than aggressive way. Assertiveness gives us the control we need in our daily lives. But many people tend to be controlled by others, or even by their own anger. This is a pattern that can quickly lead to the feeling that one's life is essentially out of control.

There are many unhealthy compensatory behaviors that people use to cope with this lack of control, which is real and not imagined. For people who develop Binge Eating Disorder, binge eating is a major manifestation. If you struggle with BED, my advice is to look at your other behaviors as well. In what other ways do you cope with the feeling of being out of control? Some binge eaters also deal with feeling out of control by self-harming, lashing out on others, engaging in compulsive sexual behaviors, or resorting to any number of actions that are harmful rather than helpful. Even if your other coping skills seem as innocuous as procrastinating, interrupt yourself if you're saying in your head, "Oh, come on. Who doesn't wait until the last minute sometimes? Life gets freaking busy!" You're right. Life does get busy, and it *can* be overwhelming. That's exactly why it's so important to recognize our stressors and triggers for harmful behaviors and develop coping mechanisms that are helpful- not harmful. (Again, we'll talk about this more in depth when we discuss cognitive behavioral therapy).

Let's get back to the emotions we repress, and how journaling can be as crucial to recovery as therapy. For both sexes, repressed emotions can lead to overeating, and journaling gives us a safe space to process our feelings before we're ready to communicate them to others. Of course, some feelings and entries may always stay private, and this makes it even more special. Journaling is also an invaluable tool in tracking connections between the actions that lead to binges. Think of your thoughts, emotions, and behaviors as intrinsically interconnected in a never-ending feedback loop.

Your thoughts influence your emotions and vice versa; both influence your behaviors. Physiologically, your thoughts and feelings continually alter your brain chemistry, which then affects everything you experience! The body/mind connection begins at birth and doesn't end until you take your last breath, and the conversations are varied and ongoing. Everyone's body/mind connection is unique, and we all respond to it in different ways. Journaling is one very useful way to track the major ways in which your body and mind connection is expressed. Personal growth results from understanding.

In addition to journaling, keep a separate record of your binge eating episodes. This is a space where you can record the times that you binge eat, what you ate, and how you felt afterward. To make this easier for you, I've put together an easy to use worksheet that you can download for free at my website

https://www.bcfpublishing.com/bingedownload

In the worksheet, you'll find a "hunger scale" that will help you score your hunger or fullness on a scale of 0 to 10, with 0 being completely starving and 10 being so full you feel as though you might explode. Each time you record a binge, also record your hunger score before and after eating, to understand how you were feeling before the binge, and the physical impact you felt after.

Feel free to make side notes in it about what triggered particular episodes so that the connection stays fresh in your mind, but you don't have to. And save the more in-depth, long-winded feelings and expressions for your journal.

Studies have shown that merely tracking your activities can make it easier to curb a bad habit like binge eating. And I've found that there's no more straightforward way to get visibility into your own behavior than keeping a simple log. You might be tempted to skip this step, after all, you know when you've binged —you don't need to write it down. But we're quick to forget, especially when memories are painful, and it can be quite a revelation to see exactly how much we're actually binging. Please, however you choose to do it, start your log today and begin tracking (and hopefully reducing) your binge eating.

The Importance of Mindful Eating in Recovery

I know we talked about it in more depth earlier, but I can't stress enough the role of mindful eating in recovery. As I said before, mindful eating is a learned behavior that doesn't become instinctive right away. In the beginning stages, and whenever you need to get back on track, it's really helpful to track how mindfully you're eating as well as binging episodes. What do I mean by this?

Let me explain. Whenever you have the time, write about a meal you ate. As you write, ask yourself the following questions: How did my body feel during and after eating this meal? Do I feel full, and am I satisfied? (Remember, those are two different things). How easily and comfortably did my body digest the foods I just ate? Write descriptively about the sensory experience of eating, too. If you cooked it, include what you liked and disliked about the recipe and work involved. Did you making this meal tap your creativity? Was it fun to make? (If not, don't worry! No one has fun *all* the time while cooking, and you'll get to a place where it's enjoyable some of the time).

Writing about your positive experiences with food helps restore the art and joy of eating and preparing food, and writing down the negative ones helps you determine what to avoid in the future. In this way, you're gradually developing the best meal plan for you without even realizing it. In the long-term, this method of meal planning is so much more realistic and reliable than dieting (not to mention much more satisfying).

By tracking your mindful eating experiences, you'll glean a clearer idea of what foods your body is responding to positively and which ones to avoid because your body just doesn't like them. You're also recording the positive with the negative, which gives you a more well-rounded, holistic perspective of the recovery process.

If you go into recovery like a chore, gloving up and preparing to get your hands dirty for the overhaul, the process will seem tedious and undesirable. You won't feel motivated every day, and there will be ups and downs, some more intense than others. It can be tempting to view recovery as we tend to see other challenges in a busy, overworked life, and just want to "get it over with." But your recovery is not a task with a beginning and an end. It's a new lifestyle to adopt for the long-term, and it ultimately brings more joy than pain. But getting to that point takes time, which is why I wrote this book —to help guide you through one of the most challenging but rewarding journeys of your life.

Respecting Your Food

All mutually beneficial relationships go both ways, including your relationship with food. Respecting yourself means developing a sense of respect for the food you eat and where it came from. Making mindful choices involves sourcing your food and understanding how and where it was grown. Was it farmed locally or from a corporate source? If the food didn't come from a local source, what are the farming practices involved with the company you are buying from? If your meal includes meat, the way the animals were raised and treated plays a big role in the quality of your food. Were the animals treated with any hormones or antibiotics? If you have chicken or eggs, were they free range or packed into tight spaces, creating risk for disease and the need for antibiotics? These topics can be hard to stomach sometimes. But asking yourself these important questions is a vital part of mindful eating and changing your toxic relationship with food. In order to respect your food and gain the most value from it, you've got to know where it comes from.

Getting the facts doesn't have to be an arduous, time-consuming process. A simple Google search of the company you're buying from, along with a little reliable word of mouth, will tell you a lot. One of the positive things happening in society regarding food is an ongoing, open conversation about health and wellness on social media. Rather than counting calories, a whole culture of people on social media is popularizing the concept of mindful eating over dieting. In fact, a cursory glance at Facebook or Instagram will reveal hundreds to thousands of body-positive social media influencers with moderate to massive followings.

The body positivity movement is as much about mindful eating as it is about loving yourself for who you are. It shifts the focus from weight to health, which is a much-needed change in this weight-obsessed culture. Provided we're discerning about facts and sources, social media groups can provide us with some social support as well as information. They can also provide tips about mindful eating, and there is a lot to be learned from sharing our experiences with others and learning about theirs. There's also a lot to be learned about the brands you buy from on social media. If you're interested in tips to help you find the healthiest, affordable food sources and buying options are available to you. Knowing what you're eating is one of the most critical parts of meal planning. This knowledge strengthens your mind and body connection in positive ways and makes it easier for you to understand your body's responses to the food you eat.

Respecting Your Wellness

I'll say it again: take your time when you eat. It allows your body to fully digest your food and get the maximum amount of nutrition the food contains. It also makes for a richer, more relaxed experience, leading to greater satisfaction. The satisfaction factor is important because the more satisfied you feel, the less likely you are to binge eat. Ask yourself how you would like to feel physically, mentally, and emotionally after eating. If you'd like to feel energized and fulfilled, make sure your food —and the way you eat —is lending itself to that goal.

We know that during episodes of binge eating, people with BED typically eat quickly and in private, almost as if they're just getting the meal or snack over with. Usually, because they feel shame and anxiety about the amount of food they are eating at once. Yet, because binge eating provides a temporary outlet for negative feelings, it brings a sense of comfort that can be addictive. When you've stopped binging behaviors and have begun to eat intuitively, notice the way you feel emotionally as well as physically. There are no wrong feelings in this process; there is only insight to be gained from taking inventory of your emotions while you eat. Do you feel calm and relaxed, or are you feeling stressed? Do you feel good or bad about yourself at this moment? Binge eating is usually an escape from negative emotions in one's life, and food is used as a crutch or avoidant behavior. Now that you've removed that crutch and can't rely on it anymore, what emotions are surfacing while you eat?

If painful or unpleasant emotions arise in relation to food, try not to view them only in relation to food. What do I mean by this? If you feel a negative emotion while eating, look inside to see where the feeling came from. For example, in the early stages, some people continue to feel shame while they eat. They feel this way even when the foods they consume are healthy and they are eating in reasonable proportions. Sometimes, the shame of having BED for years leaves a lingering imprint and is associated with past traumas such as being mocked for being overweight in high school or ridiculed by family, etc. In some cases, the shame is not necessarily about eating, but about the emotions that binge eating kept at bay.

Let's suppose your binge eating started after a traumatic event. In a situation like this, stopping the binge eating behavior is likely to bring that trauma to the surface because you let go of the habit that seemingly has protected you from the bad feelings associated with repressed trauma. When this happens, respect your emotions. Respect your right to feel them, and just sit with them. Reach out for support from your therapist or a trusted friend or family member. There may be times when you don't even need to talk about the pain; you just need someone to sit and be with you until the negative feelings pass. That is okay, too.

Respecting your wellness doesn't just mean stopping harmful behaviors like binge eating. It also means being kind to yourself in the moments when it's the most difficult to do so. For people with BED, any food-related activity can bring up these feelings and insecurities. During these times, you will be challenged to make a choice. You can make a hasty retreat from the pain of these emotions by binge eating or resist the urge and find other, healthier ways to comfort yourself. If you choose the second again and again, it will eventually become as instinctive as your binge eating once was. Change takes time, so be patient with yourself and keep respecting your wellness. Remind yourself that you're doing great, and you deserve all of the kindness, love, and healing energy you are giving to yourself.

CHAPTER 5

Managing Stress In New, Healthy Ways

"You are braver than you believe, and stronger than you seem, and smarter than you think."

– Christopher Robin

We talked a lot about the effects of stress on Binge Eating Disorder, but now we're going to discuss stress management in depth. Just as changing your toxic relationship with food requires you to implement skill sets, behaviors, and ways of thinking, so does changing the way you manage stress. Transforming the way you handle stress only in relation to eating would be fruitless and wouldn't give you the tools you need to avoid binge eating in the long-term. Relieving stress, in general, helps reduce the need to binge for people with BED, so my next step is to help you build a system for managing stress that works for you.

The first step is to identify the major stressors in your life and come up with new, more effective ways to manage them. Actually, that's two steps. Let's focus on the first part now. We talked extensively about potential stressors in the first chapter of this book. For me, the biggest ones stemmed from trying to maintain an overwhelming schedule, not having enough time for myself, resulting in a lack of self-care. Another was low self-esteem and difficulty communicating with my loved ones, which, of course, led to more binge eating. My life had been trapped in that cycle for as long as I could remember, and the time had come to ask myself what I needed to be able to break it. Now I'm asking you to ask yourself the same question. What are your biggest sources of stress, and what do you need from yourself and others to overcome them? Are your most significant stressors related to time management, relationships, trauma, career, children, health and wellness, or other things?

Whatever the sources of your stress, don't count Binge Eating Disorder as one them. Yes, it's a major source of stress! But more to the point, it's a reaction to your stressors. This does not make you good or bad; the truth is far more simple. It's that you are overly stressed and need help to manage that stress in order to make some necessary changes in your life. You are far from alone in this. In fact, my other book *Stress Relief for the Anxious Mind* goes into more depth about stress and its effects on the body and mind. It guides you through the process of implementing healthy stress management skills in your daily life.

When it comes to being busy, I hear you. Having an active life and career in itself is not a problem and can be a sign of a full, thriving life. It only becomes a problem when your energy is pulled in so many directions that you become depleted, and there is no time or strength left for self-care or personal growth. Balance is the key to adequate stress management. Usually, the solution to this problem is time management, which we'll cover more about shortly. For now, let's talk about how you use your time and energy. After all, these two things are two of the most precious commodities you'll ever own.

Contrary to what you may believe when you're stretched too thin and living more for others than yourself, you do own your time and energy. They belong first and foremost to you, even when you have children. If you find that your first instinct is to object wildly to this, factor this into the equation: a healthy parent's first instinct is usually to care for his or her child before the self; it's a biologically ingrained mechanism that has preserved many species over time, including ours! So it's natural and right to feel that your children come first. However, you are just as important as they are. In fact, if you have children, putting yourself first is a way of prioritizing your children's needs. If you're physically and emotionally drained of your resources, it becomes harder to give your children the physical and emotional support they need in their own development. The balancing act is not easy, and time and stress management is not always a linear path. There are setbacks for everyone, but what's important is that you learn how to overcome them and build resiliency over time.

While we're on the topic, let's touch a bit on building time management skills. Time management is actually a set of multiple skills, so let's go over it step-by-step. I strongly recommend starting by writing a list of the things you absolutely have to do during the week. A list of things that definitely can't be done at a later date, such as completing certain work projects, going shopping for things your children need for school, cooking dinner, etc. Prioritizing is key to time management. You don't have to strictly regiment your time to manage it efficiently (in fact, this can cause more stress). Just set specific short- and long-term goals for yourself and set reasonable deadlines on them. Making use of your time in a way that serves your goals is one of the most important stress management skills you will ever learn.

Just like we talked about eating mindfully and taking our time, the same goes for accomplishing goals. Even though the kind of goals we're talking about now are concrete ones with fixed or flexible deadlines, you want to set goals that make you feel good. In the beginning stages of my recovery, I stumbled over a lot of my goals. With the blissful ignorance of one writing down goals for the first time, I would jot away, beaming with pride at my own efficacy: "See Lauren, that wasn't so hard! Look at you, writing down your goals like a beast." But then, suddenly, I would stop. At the prospect of actually accomplishing them, I'd find myself paralyzed with anxiety. Turns out, writing down goals is a lot different than actually doing them.

When this happens, stop and reevaluate your goals. Determine what about them makes you so anxious. If it's an unrealistic or overwhelming deadline, see if you can modify it. If it's a project that involves outlining, planning, or writing, take a second look at what you've written. Did you stuff it all into one weekend, one in which you also happened to be squeezing in a visit from intolerable in-laws or, say, all the errands you didn't have time to do during the week? If so, that goal isn't a realistic one. It might be more sensible to take an hour or two per night to work on the project. Access your focus. Some people do really well cramming long-winded projects into small amounts of time; that can be great if it works for you. Others have less concentration prowess and need to divide tasks into smaller windows of time, and that's great, too. The objective is to get to know yourself and what you need, then plan accordingly. You can take back control of your time and your life with a little planning —and a commitment to stick to the plan.

Goal-setting and managing time also encompasses long-term goals that are measured more by satisfaction than by deadlines. Without these, life loses its meaning, depression sets in, and you lack the motivation to complete even your simple tasks. All of this contributes to a pervasive sense of powerlessness and the belief that your life is out of your control. "Everything else is a mess, so is it really so important to stick to my meal plan or deny myself a few more pieces of cake?" If that sounds familiar to you, take a deeper look inside.

It takes time, but an open heart will eventually lead you to the things that are most important to you in life. If you're single and one of your deepest wishes is to share an intimate, satisfying connection with a partner, why not make that a goal for yourself? Sure, there are no deadlines or guarantees when it comes to happiness in love. But setting goals that help free your time and energy up for opportunity is important if you'd like to be in a fulfilling relationship. What past traumas, harmful beliefs, or unhealthy habits do you need to release before being psychologically ready to maintain a healthy intimate relationship? If you have a career goal that has not been realized, what steps do you need to take to get there? What self-limiting beliefs can you overcome now?

Prioritization and time management are skills you need for both short- and long-term goals. Another benefit of prioritizing your goals is that doing so eliminates the goals that never should have been on your list, to begin with. When you take time to reflect on what your priorities actually are, you realize what they aren't. It becomes clearer which short-term goals serve the long-term goals you have for your life.

Self-Awareness is Key

When you know what's truly important to you in life, you can set your short-term goals around your long-term goals. As you journal, your deepest desires will gradually be apparent on the pages in front of you. It can be immensely overwhelming to know what you want but have no idea how to get it. Just this anxiety alone can paralyze you, causing you to detach from your feelings and head to the refrigerator for comfort. (Again, it's okay for food to provide comfort, but when it's your primary source of it, eating becomes an avoidant behavior that escalates into excess). So if you feel overwhelmed by goal setting, set a few at a time. Or walk away from the task and come back to it later. Sometimes, dissociation or the urge to binge eat is your body telling you that it's under too much pressure to function optimally at the moment. Honor the message your body is sending you and return to your goals later. In the meantime, try to do something relaxing, like watching a movie you've been wanting to see or taking a brief nap. If you can't do something relaxing at the moment, plan on it at one point during the day or night.

When you do come back to your goals and start working toward them, exercise self-awareness. There are no real limits to the ways in which your likes, dislikes, and needs can affect your work. They affect your interests and strengths and areas for improvement, as well as the way you interact with others. They affect your behavior and the conditions you need to perform at your best. That's where journaling comes in (yes, again). Any time you feel you've performed at your best or feel really good while doing a task, identify the specific reasons for it. What about your environment motivated, energized, or relaxed you enough to sharpen your focus? What was your state of mind? If calm and focused, was it the result or prioritizing, goal setting, and planning? Was it the result of a positive attitude about work? In other words, write down what you're doing right, and do it again. And again.

In the same vein, record what you're doing wrong for you. (Keep in mind that what's wrong for you might be totally right for another as everyone is different). This can range from simple to profound and complex, but no detail is too small. If you worked at a desk and opened a window to let a little sunlight in, and you noticed this improved your mood or focus, write that down.

Speaking of the seemingly small stuff, I highly recommend making a list of things you'd like to do for yourself just this week. Include things you don't think you have the time to do and would ordinarily not even consider as part of your agenda. It can be as simple as doing something you want with your hair or taking a long, hot bath. It can include writing your thoughts and feelings in a journal, meditating, or other activities that help recenter and recharge your core energy. Create a list of activities that make you feel good and see how many of them you can fit in when you manage your time more adequately.

CHAPTER 6

Adapting to a Healthier Lifestyle

"The more you adapt, the more interesting you are."
– Martha Stewart

Getting Adequate Exercise and Sleep

Although not all people with Binge Eating Disorder are overweight, many are. Being overweight or obese can present specific challenges in terms of exercise and physical activity. On a physical level, there may be comorbid health problems that make it difficult or uncomfortable to exercise. If this is the case, talk to a healthcare provider before starting a new physical activity routine. Many people with BED feel little to no motivation to engage in physical activity. There may be physical and emotional reasons for this. If it's been a while since you've wanted to or been able to exercise, your body may be somewhat deconditioned. Deconditioning is a complex physiological change in the body following a long period of inactivity, and it happens at various levels. In moderate to severe cases, it can involve functional losses in the ability to accomplish daily tasks.

Deconditioning affects the body in many different ways. Cardiac health is impacted by a decrease in cardiac output. There is also decreased blood pressure in upright positions, which often results in faster heart rates both with activity and with rest. (This is a problem that can be intensely exacerbated by physical activity). Depending on the severity of deconditioning, it can also be associated with decreased lung function. Muscles may become contracted or even atrophied over time, and there might even be reduced muscle density (although this happens in severe cases and is often associated with prolonged bed rest or morbid obesity).

If you're experiencing difficulty tolerating exercise, you'll need to start out slowly. If you tolerate exercise reasonably well, you might be able to begin with a more intense routine. Whatever your abilities, it's important to start somewhere. But just like with meal plans, there's no "one size fits all" when it comes to physical activity or exercise routines. The routine that works best for you depends on many different factors, including your health, lifestyle, and preferences.

Yoga can also be an effective way to relax and realign your energies while burning calories for weight loss. Recent studies have shown that yoga can help women struggling with binge eating. Regular routines, including postures, breathing, and relaxation techniques, and meditation, can lead to less binge eating, higher self-esteem, and a more positive body image for people with BED. The theories vary, but part of the answer probably lies in the link between stress and binge eating. Yoga gives people with BED different, more positive ways to handle stress. We feel more in control when we can breathe through our stress. Doing yoga, along with meditation, helps us stay calm through anxiety. Sometimes stress occurs when we don't have the balance we need to cope with triggering situations. Yoga and meditation, which balances our energies, can help us become more resilient.

Yoga, meditation, and relaxation exercises also help people with BED sit in a safe space with uncomfortable emotions rather than escaping from them by binge eating. When it comes to unpleasant feelings, we can't dodge them or "beat around the bush," as the saying goes. We've got to go through them, but we need a comfortable way to do so. Many yoga practices emphasize mindfulness and acceptance of thoughts and feelings without judgment. Your emotions are not good or bad; they just are.

For some people, starting with gentle yoga is the best way to get to know your body and experiment with movement. Yoga also helps use the body to relieve stress in positive ways. Using your body as a powerful tool for stress relief leads to more confidence and better self-esteem. It also helps you feel more in control of your life. You may start to think, "I don't have to overeat to relieve my stress; I can use my own body to meet my needs while I am anxious." You might not be used to seeing your body as a tool for stress relief, but it's one of the most powerful, accessible ones you've got at your disposal.

Any form of exercise you enjoy can help in your recovery from BED. Again, by doing something physical that you love, you're relating to your body in a positive way. Exercise such as walking, running, or doing aerobic activity has its own unique benefits that aid in the recovery of BED. When you exercise, you're tapping into your reserve of strength and energy to take control over stress and urges to overeat. Be mindful when you exercise. Notice the way your heart accelerates, your skin perspires, and your muscles tense and release themselves.

Yoga is a form of exercise that encourages awareness of the body and mind connection. Once you become aware of how your body feels when you have certain emotions, you can use yoga to help you relieve the stress or pain you're feeling. When negative emotions bring on cravings, try a yoga pose or relaxation exercise instead of making a beeline to the freezer. With time, the emotion and cravings will pass by with more and more ease. When this happens, you know you've replaced a negative habit with a positive one, and that is no small feat!

There are many mindful meditations and relaxation techniques that encourage you to tense and then release your muscles. The conscious sensations of building and releasing tension in your body is a powerful outlet for stress. You can feel negative emotions filling your body, and then let them go. Many people with Binge Eating Disorder either consciously or subconsciously view their bodies as the enemy, not an ally. They experience their body as out of control and learn to hate it because of this. Some people overcompensate for these feelings by exercising beyond their limits and growing too weak to be physical again in the near future. But many with BED end up avoiding exercise altogether for the most part.

Although exercise can certainly help people with BED reconnect to their bodies in a positive way, it's important to note that exercise alone cannot lead to recovery from the disorder. In fact, making only physical changes and avoiding the emotions that trigger binge eating is extremely unhealthy and harmful to people with BED. Also, appropriate levels of exercise vary from person to person and can change from one point of recovery to the next. I recommend starting slowly if you haven't exercised in a long time and tire easily. But it's important to consult a trusted medical doctor and mental health professional before deciding on an exercise plan that's right for you. The professionals in your life can provide insights and help you form the best plan for your recovery. Remember, that plan can always be modified at the appropriate time.

As with eating, listen mindfully to your body while you exercise. How do your muscles feel? Do they feel weak and depleted or strong and energized? A lot of people talk about "good pain" and "bad pain" in terms of exercise. "Good pain" should mean that you're feeling muscle strain from physical effort, but it's tolerable and feels okay to keep going. When you exercise within your body's limits and eat meals high in protein before, and after, your body will use it to recover in a timely manner. But if you're overexerting yourself, recovery will take much longer, and you will feel fatigued. So, listen to your body while exercising. It's good to push past resistance to some extent; that's what helps you overcome barriers and build endurance over time. But overextending and pushing past the point of tolerance will result in a setback.

If you experience a setback, don't beat yourself up about it or give up. Many people with BED have low self-esteem, and some have a poor body image. For these reasons and more, they get easily discouraged when exercise causes discomfort. We'll talk about how to handle those feelings in a moment. For now, I want to help you understand the ways in which exercise is important for people with BED.

Being physically active is important because getting enough exercise can reduce the risk of chronic diseases and can potentially prevent some cancers, heart disease, osteoporosis, Type 2 diabetes, and many more. Regular exercise is associated with a drastic decrease in cardiovascular mortality and is integral to the health of the circulatory system as well. It helps prevent high blood pressure and lowers it over time in people who already have it. If you have trouble sleeping, exercise contributes to more restorative rest.

A lot of people with Binge Eating Disorder have anxiety about exercising, so let's process this together. Aside from the anxiety surrounding the physical stress of physical activity, including health problems, many people with BED also have emotional fears about exercise. What are some of the common sources of this emotional anxiety? Well, there are a number of common triggers. People who are overweight or obese and have BED might feel that they don't fit in at the gym; they may fear that they'll become a target of negative attention regarding their appearance. This self-consciousness seriously inhibits many people who are overweight, causing severe enough anxiety or depression to prevent them from exercising in front of others (or at all).

People who have been overweight for a long time may have painful memories of being teased, bullied, or feeling embarrassed in school or PE class. While some people use this feeling of shame as a motivator to overcome obesity or inactivity (e.g., I'm sick and tired of being ashamed of myself, so I'm going to lose this weight right now!"), it's also important to find ways to make peace with your body right now. When shame is their motivator, people with BED usually end up either falling back into the same patterns or manifesting new unhealthy behaviors. Of course, there's nothing wrong with being proud of yourself and the way you look when you lose weight. But deeper self-love, a love of the person you are on the inside —requires that you learn to choose self-love and compassion at any stage, even if you haven't lost any weight yet.

There is a lot of stigma surrounding obesity in our society, which perpetuates the false generalization that overweight people are lazy or gluttonous. We live in a fat-phobic society that attaches a stigma to those who struggle to maintain their weight. Unfortunately, many overweight people have been the target of discrimination, bullying, or abuse about their size. This can lead to very low self-esteem and paralyzing anxiety about exercise. Yet, it's important to find ways to manage the anxiety so that you can reap the health benefits of exercise and avoid or reduce the risk of comorbid conditions associated with BED.

Your anxiety may not go away entirely or immediately, and that's okay. What's important is to learn to manage it in ways that help you push through the anxiety and find a physical activity routine that's right for you. One way to do this is to make sure you don't exceed your limits. If you haven't been exercising regularly, a little bit of tiredness or strain at the beginning is normal. Start slowly and build your exercise tolerance gradually rather than pushing yourself so hard that it results in counterproductive exhaustion or muscle fatigue. Even five or ten minutes per day is a good starting point if your tolerance is low. It's important to treat your body with patience and kindness and listen when it tells you that it's had enough. If you're in pain beyond normal muscle strain from exertion or you're feeling fatigued, then it really is counterproductive to continue. Pushing yourself too far will usually only result in the inability to be active the next time exercise is on your schedule, which can be frustrating and make you feel worse emotionally. Pushing yourself beyond your body's limits also causes you, at least subconsciously, to associate exercise or physical activity with pain and discomfort. I can feel my motivation draining just thinking about it! It's much healthier to respect your wellness, which means respecting your body's limits when it comes to both eating and exercise. Doing this will help avoid burnout and maximize the health benefits of exercise.

There is no amount of exercise that is too small at the beginning; what matters is that you're making an effort to improve your health and change your habits. Allow yourself to be proud and take joy from it! If you've been afraid or unmotivated when it comes to exercise, then just getting yourself to begin is a monumental step. Over time, you will build endurance and gain more physical and emotional confidence about exercising.

When I first started increasing my exercise levels, I knew I had to do something to improve my motivation during times when I was feeling physically or emotionally sluggish. I made a point of listening to my body when I felt that my body needed rest more than it needed exercise. (There definitely were days like that, and there will be for you, too. This is normal, and you should listen to your body's instincts). But in order to keep on track, you'll probably be like me and need a little extra motivation factor sometimes. One way that I did this was to reward myself when I pushed through my reluctance.

Although I believe in indulging in moderation, try not to make your reward for exercising food-related. The reason for this is that, ideally, you'll want to make exercise enjoyable on its own, independent of food rewards. The other purpose is that associating exercise with food rewards may exacerbate the tendency to rationalize binge eating. Not everyone with BED will do this, but because the cravings associated with the disorder can be so intense, many people have formed a long-term habit of rationalizing their over-eating. Especially in the beginning stages of recovery, rewarding yourself with non-food-related things is a safer bet. Again, this is not because you shouldn't give into temptation with regard to moderation. Just don't relate it to exercise until you feel as if you've truly recovered, and doing so won't cause a setback. Instead, do something else you enjoy. Treat yourself to a night out, or a night in front of the TV doing nothing. Buy yourself a new outfit if this week's budget allows. Just make sure your reward is genuinely satisfying to you; after all, a boring reward isn't going to get you out of bed and into the gym (or wherever you exercise) on Monday morning!

Another effective way to push through exercise anxiety is to do it in a place where you feel comfortable. If that's at home in the privacy of your own living room, that's exactly where you should be. If the variety of choices and equipment at the gym make you feel motivated, then that's the best place for you. Everyone has different likes and dislikes when it comes to exercise. For me, pairing exercise with relaxation was particularly helpful when my tiredness or lack of motivation stemmed from stress. To clear my mind, I would plan thirty-minute walks in a local park. Temporarily disconnecting from others and the chaos of day-to-day life can be highly reenergizing.

Incorporating something you enjoy into your exercise plan is one of the best ways to overcome anxiety and make physical activity a more positive experience. There are options for people who would love to learn dance, yoga, or any number of physical hobbies, but can't seem to overcome their self-consciousness in groups where they are more overweight than other members of the class. There are many great online networks and resources for those who struggle with weight gain and are working to lose it. Sometimes taking an exercise, dance, or yoga class with others your size whom you can relate to helps relieve some of the shame and anxiety. Again, this may not be something you struggle with, but if it is, consider finding a group where you can exercise with people your size.

If you're unsure about finding an activity you enjoy, ask yourself a few basic questions. What kind of movement do I enjoy most? What type of setting do I prefer to move in? Do I like being on the ground or in the water? Am I artistically inclined with an interest in dance or lyrical movement, or am I more into sports and athletic activities? Do you prefer to exercise with people or alone? If it's been a while since you've been physically active, recall the activities you enjoyed as a child. There are likely some things you did that you could enjoy again.

If you're facing a lot of difficulties getting started, consider these tips for building exercise tolerance in small ways throughout the day. If you have a choice between the stairs and the elevator, take the stairs. If your work or learning space allows it, take five minute walks through the building. Stretching activities at night have multiple benefits; they can be relaxing, help you sleep better and prepare you for more exercise in the near future.

The confidence and support of family and friends can really help with exercise anxiety. While many of us are lucky to have at least one or two truly supportive people in our lives, not everyone reacts to our lifestyle changes in ways that are helpful. More often than not, people who say or do things that worsen our anxiety are well-intentioned, but not sensitive to the problems associated with BED. For example, you may have friends or family members who push you harder or faster than you can go as you progress. They may be doing this because they care and want you to succeed, but the overall impact of their words and attitudes is more harmful than helpful to someone with BED. If your friends and family are saying or doing things that hinder more than they help your progress, draw on your new communication skills, and be assertive. You can say something like, "I know you're only trying to help me, but it's healthier for me to move at my own pace, and I'd like you to respect my decision."

If setting this boundary doesn't stop the behavior, consider setting it more firmly: "I've already told you that this advice isn't helpful to me, so please don't try to give it to me again." If that doesn't change their behavior, consider disengaging from this person as much as possible, at least in terms of sharing your struggle with and recovery from BED. Even if they mean well, they may be merely incapable of or unwilling to understand your experience and respect your boundaries. Continuing to be closely involved, especially at an emotional level, with someone behaving this way could be very damaging to your recovery.

You are likely to be in a vulnerable emotional and psychological state during at least some points of your recovery from BED, especially at the beginning stages. The changes you are making will bring up difficult emotions, and you'll need a support system aligned with your needs and goals. If you don't have this kind of support from family and friends, you'll need to reach out for help from a therapist, counselor, and/or an external support system. (There will be much more information about this a little later in this book, and I will guide you through the process of finding help).

Getting back to exercise, specifically, the main points I'd like you to take away from this section are: It's okay to start slowly and work realistically within the parameters of your capabilities. I know it can be hard, but do your best to relate to yourself with love and kindness. Show yourself patience and empathy when you struggle. Don't be afraid to reach out for help and support in finding an exercise plan or class that is enjoyable to you. If you're overweight and this means exercising with similarly-sized people, that's more than okay, and there are many options available to you!

Take Control of Your Sleep Patterns

Let's talk a little bit about adequate sleep. Studies have shown that poor sleep duration and poor sleep continuity are associated with lower levels of self-regulation in eating. We don't know exactly why this is, but many psychologists agree that stress is likely a strong factor. We know that poorly-managed or overwhelming stress is often a trigger for BED. Further studies have shown increased morning levels of cortisol in people with BED, and the severity of BED symptoms is associated with this excess cortisol production. When we lack restorative sleep, our brain does not functioning optimally, and our stress tolerance decreases. Lack of sleep hurts the cognitive processes involved in attention, alertness, reasoning, concentration, and problem-solving. It presents challenges in learning and critical thinking. We know that over time, chronic insomnia or untreated sleep disorders can contribute to heart attack, heart disease, and even heart failure. It can also lead to an irregular heartbeat, high blood pressure, diabetes, and stroke.

If these symptoms sound familiar, we discussed them earlier in this book as comorbid problems associated with BED. Not only is BED positively related to poor sleep patterns, but the risk for health problems associated with BED are exacerbated and increased with poor sleep. That's why it's important to get adequate rest. If you suffer from insomnia, you might be reading this at 3:00 a.m. thinking, "Okay, yeah, better sleep sounds good. But how the heck do I get it?" But you have more control over your sleep patterns than you might think.

I'd like to share a few tips that helped me regulate my sleep during the recovery process. Because my sleep habits were out of whack, I started going to sleep and waking up at the same time every day whenever I could. (Of course, there will always be exceptions, but overall I was able to reset my internal clock so that my body got used to a balanced sleep schedule). Now that my body was on a sleep schedule, I could experience restorative sleep at more or less the same time every night, which helped increase my energy levels. If you've had a busy night and are getting to bed late, it may be tempting to sleep in. But a better option is to wake up at the same time you always do and then take an afternoon nap. This way, there's less of a chance that your sleep schedule will be disturbed.

This next tip may seem too simple to make a big difference, but I promise it's not. You want to consciously manage your exposure to light. A natural hormone, melatonin, is controlled by light exposure and helps regulate the sleep-wake cycle. But many factors in modern life, including overwhelming amounts of work and poor time management, can disturb the natural circadian rhythm.

Try to spend time outdoors during the day so you can maximize your exposure to natural light, energizing your body. Be active enough so that you feel tired at night. If it's not an option to spend time outdoors during the day, let as much light into your home or working space as possible. Open windows or blinds and sit close to the window.

Here's one that a lot of people struggle with, including me. Ideally, it's a good idea to avoid screens within 1-2 hours of bedtime. Because we often take our work home with us or rely heavily on social media and emails for business purposes, this can be more challenging than it sounds. If you must use screens right up until bed, then minimize the stimulating effect of the lights by opting for smaller screens, turning the brightness down on your phone or tablet, or even using light-altering software. The "blue light" from screens is what keeps us awake. Did you know that there are apps and features that dim the blue light at night to reduce its effects on your sleep? It's all about avoiding overstimulation prior to bedtime so that your sleep rhythms are not disturbed.

Eating and sleep are intrinsically connected. If your diet is high in caffeine or nicotine, it can cause sleep problems up to twelve hours after consumption. You also want to avoid eating large meals at night because digestion can cause stomach discomfort and heartburn. It may seem like a nice, relaxing idea to have a glass of wine before bed, but in reality, alcohol intake is only a quick fix for sleep problems that doesn't last through the night. Once you've fallen asleep, alcohol causes sleep disturbances while you're out. You should also make it a point to avoid eating refined sugar and carbohydrates frequently throughout the day. These foods can trigger wakefulness at night and even disrupt the deep, restorative stages of sleep.

As discussed, eating and exercise are highly interconnected. Exercise speeds up metabolism, stimulates cortisol production, and elevates body temperature — all processes that use the body's energy throughout the day so that sleep comes more easily at night. That said, you'll want to avoid vigorous exercise within three hours before bedtime. If you exercise too close to bedtime, your metabolism and cortisol production will be operating at their peak, preventing restful sleep.

Low-impact exercise, such as yoga or stretching, can facilitate restful sleep. These are the exercises you can safely do before bed. Recovering from BED involves working in harmony with your body's natural rhythms. People with BED tend to fight these rhythms, pushing themselves past their physical and mental limits in order to fulfill their responsibilities and succeed. The stress of it becomes too much, and soon we're not only binge eating to escape from our poorly managed stress, but we also lack the energy required to make healthy decisions about food. This cycle exacerbates the feeling of loss of control, ultimately leading to more binge eating. But yoga can give us the skills to cope with whatever we are feeling rather than escaping into food for pain and stress relief. It's well-known that people with eating disorders, including people with BED or who are overweight, have a tendency to dissociate from their bodies. Dissociation usually happens on a subconscious level when we don't want to face what we're feeling. Sometimes it's anger that threatens to overcome us, and we're afraid that if we let it out our, we will be out of control. Sometimes we hold anger in because we don't think that anyone around us will listen to or understand our feelings. We know by now that depression is one of the most intense triggers for BED because its hallmark is a pervasive sense of hopelessness, making us feel a lack of control of our own thoughts and moods.

Along with therapy, medical treatment, and sometimes psychiatric treatment, yoga is a powerful tool of recovery. It makes the connection between our bodies and minds, helping us understand the emotional context behind certain physical sensations and discomfort. It's worth repeating that people who binge eat often feel very desperate when they do. They simply cannot tolerate the emotional pain anymore, and they need to feel relief right now. But through low-stress, relaxing exercise, yoga gently prompts us to sit with our feelings and listen to what our bodies need. Is it more exercise, more rest or to work fewer hours in a row? Are we feeling lonely and needing to spend more time with family and friends? Before I learned to manage my time in a way that worked for and not against my wellness, I often had the physical sensation that my energy was being snatched from me. It was as if someone had reached into my energy space and was eating away at it in chunks! Sounds pretty intense, right? Well, I was functioning on autopilot for so long that I got used to sensations like this. They became my new normal until the stress built up until I reached a breaking point. Yoga took me off autopilot and helped me live in the moment.

When you're going through daily life on autopilot, usually that means you're eating on autopilot, too. You're detached from the experience of eating; you're not really savoring or feeling the taste or texture of the food, or the way it makes your body feel. You also don't necessarily feel it when you're full. You've lost connection to what you are eating, and it ultimately becomes a form of escape that offers only short-lived relief. No matter how many times you run away from a problem, whether, with binge eating or other avoidant behaviors, the problem will keep resurfacing.

Yoga is one way to meet the causes of your stress head-on and find real solutions for them. Your body and mind connection is enhanced during yoga, so if you listen to your body, you will gradually learn more and more about where and why it is hurting. You will slowly come to know why you are binge eating and how you can stop. Yoga uses various postures, breathing exercises, relaxation techniques, and meditation to help restore the body/mind connection and align your energies. It helps facilitate non-judgmental awareness and puts you in a place of acceptance of your thoughts, sensations, and emotions. In this way, yoga challenges the tendency to escape through food by offering a new, healthier coping mechanism.

Through controlled breathing, yoga helps restore your body/mind connection. It can create a pause between a craving and an overeating behavior. In that pause, you might say to yourself, "I am feeling intolerably stressed right now, but I food is not my only way to manage stress. I can also breathe and stretch through this craving, and it will pass. Nothing lasts forever. My stress will also pass." Doing this, again and again, shows your body that it doesn't need food for stress relief, and even your physiologically induced cravings will diminish in intensity over time.

Remember, recovery from Binge Eating Disorder involves a complete lifestyle change, not just a change in your eating habits. Many people typically address their eating habits and put themselves on a meal plan without dealing with the underlying emotional causes of BED. This is counterproductive. If we don't learn how to self-soothe, cope with our pain, and manage our time and stress, the urge to binge eat will persist.

That's why I take a holistic approach to recovery and want to help you take one, too.

By tapping you into your body's natural resources for stress relief, joy, and fulfillment, yoga also teaches self-love. In many respects, the discipline is a way of relating to your body with compassion, transcending the shame and guilt triggered by overeating. Once you learn even the simplest yoga or meditation routine, you can turn to that routine if you've recently binged or are feeling desperately close to doing so.

Instead of beating yourself up about binge eating or strong urges, yoga helps you find where the urge came from. It encourages you to breathe and stretch through the pain and stress. Many meditation exercises, used in and out of the realm of yoga, prompt you to strategically tense your muscles, then let the tension go, feeling it drain out of the body parts holding so much of it. Think of your body like a sponge. It absorbs not just your own stress and emotions, but the stress and feelings of people around you to a degree. In order to set energetic boundaries and prevent yourself from becoming drained, you can learn meditative exercises that will release negativity with and without yoga. Self-compassion stops the binge-eating cycle in its tracks by transcending shame and self-flagellation. It provides another, more nurturing way to cope with stress and pain.

Find the Right Type of Yoga for You

Hatha is the most common type of yoga practiced in the United States. It's offered at almost every yoga studio, gym, or class. It involves holding specific positions for limited amounts of time. However, yin yoga is a kind that requires individuals to hold poses for extended lengths of time. It helps build stress tolerance and challenges people to face their discomfort, to go inside and feel the parts of the body and mind connection that are out of alignment. As time goes by and your tolerance builds up, you'll be able to hold poses for longer and meditate through your stress triggers. Even better, you'll take home the awareness of your body gleaned from yoga. You'll be aware of when you're hurting and what you need when you're stressed or hurt.

Although exercise alone can relieve stress, yoga combines physical fitness with an emotional philosophy of self-awareness and compassion. A portion of a person with BED's stress is rooted in self-loathing. People with BED are commonly very hard on themselves, which leads them to overeat for temporarily stress relief. Yoga can help interrupt this cycle because its philosophy involves being kind and non-judgmental toward oneself and others.

CHAPTER 7

Healthy Mind, Healthy Life

"No body is worth more than your body"
– Melody Carstairs

How Cognitive Behavioral Therapy Can Help

Many people who struggle with eating disorders, including BED, benefit substantially from Cognitive Behavioral Therapy. Cognitive Behavioral Therapy has actually become the most popular kind of psychotherapy to treat BED. It operates on the premise that an individual's thoughts, feelings, and behaviors are interconnected and can be re-structured to support more productive ones. I love CBT because it draws from the concept of neuroplasticity. It provides us with ways to control our body/mind connection rather than having it control us.

There are three phases of treatment in CBT: the behavioral phase, the cognitive phase, and the maintenance and relapse phase. During the behavioral phase, the patient and clinician focus on building their relationship and establishing trust. Once a comfortable rapport is established, the clinician/therapist encourages the patient to identify negative emotions that lead to negative eating behaviors. The clinician then helps the patient formulate a plan for normalizing eating behaviors. (Using intuitive eating to put together a meal plan is part of this process). In this stage, the clinician will help provide educational and awareness resources about the benefits of balanced eating and nutrition.

The patient will also learn healthier coping strategies to rely on when the urge to binge becomes intense. Replacing negative behaviors with positive ones takes time and practice, but it ultimately works. It also supports the concept of neuroplasticity by proving that altered behaviors lead to new brain connections that influence feelings and thoughts. In the same vein, thoughts influence feelings and behaviors. (By now, you've probably got a clearer picture of how fluid and active the mind/body connection is throughout every day).

In the cognitive phase of CBT, patients are able to challenge their thought processes and identify unhealthy thoughts or belief systems that trigger binge eating. The clinician helps them reframe and reshape their thoughts by gaining new perspectives. As just one example, a friend who had a health issue that required specialized treatment. She ended up having to think outside the box and seek help from out of state, and the travel costs and physical illness were immensely stressful. She would sometimes think, "I can't believe things got so bad I had to seek help out of my own state." But then she would reframe this thought with a more positive perspective: "This may be difficult, but this situation gave me the opportunity to work with a medical group who is very familiar with my particular problem, which is often misunderstood."

That's an extreme example, but it shows us that it is possible to reframe our thoughts, sometimes even in devastating situations. When we do think more positively, it stimulates the brain to make "feel-good" hormones and utilize energy more efficiently. Reframing negative thoughts with positive perspectives also gives us a feeling of control over our lives and minimizes the "fight or flight" stress response that depletes the body systems.

An unrealistic level of perfectionism exists in our society. It's a fact that many of us are working to change by sharing our recovery from eating disorders and positive experiences with CBT. Sharing our personal, often painful experiences with eating disorders, as well as talking about recovery, is one way of fighting the perfectionism that still exists strongly in our weight-obsessed culture. Sometimes, feeling as if you're a part of the solution for healing a problem is therapeutic on its own; it certainly helps build self-esteem and support systems that help us overcome the negative beliefs about our bodies that society instills in us.

Cognitive Behavioral Therapy guides us through the process of acknowledging that the media represents unrealistic beauty ideals. These media images produce and exacerbate the florid distortions in our self-perceptions. How many times have you encountered a person whose stomach is normal-sized or even small, but the person becomes obsessed with trimming down because it "hangs over when she sits"? Well, to a degree, your stomach is actually supposed to come over your pants when you sit down, and there's nothing wrong with it. It doesn't mean you need to push against your body's limits to do excessive exercise routines and build muscle in the area.

If you're very into strength training or an athlete, working out vigorously to build muscle makes sense as long as you do it in a healthy way. But while recovering from Binge Eating Disorder, I don't recommend intense, challenging exercise routines until you feel that you have essentially recovered. Before you take on an intensive exercise program, it's very important to overcome your toxic relationship with food and start building a new one. This takes time and effort. One of the biggest myths the fad diet industry has perpetuated is that there is such a thing as an overnight cure or a quick fix to binge eating. There is not. Recovery from BED happens when we leave dieting behind and rely intuitively on our bodies to tell us what we need to function optimally.

CBT identifies the body distortions we've developed through unrealistic portrayals of perfection in the media. It also helps us identify the body distortions we've developed based on our own emotions and personal experiences. We might have a parent who continually obsessed about our weight, or we binge eat to relieve ourselves from emotional pain we're not ready to deal with. I have a friend whose family is very loving and supportive in most respects. But my friend's parents have always told her, "it's a shame she's overweight because otherwise, she's very beautiful." As a result of internalizing this powerful message, my friend grew up hating herself for her weight and believing that her natural beauty was canceled out by the fact that she struggled with maintaining a normal weight. The emotional distress caused by hating herself caused her to "yo-yo" diet for many years. She would radically restrict herself, followed by long periods of binge eating and was never able to maintain a balanced weight.

I want to take time to emphasize something: The cognitive distortions associated with BED require professional help and support to overcome. CBT helps us embrace a more realistic body image that can be attained by implementing a healthy meal plan. It also helps us realize that self-worth is contingent on who we are as people, not what we weigh. The idea that self-esteem is dependent on how much we weigh is a societal distortion. CBT breaks down that distortion for us, helping us embrace new perspectives about food and body image.

CBT also helps people with BED improve interpersonal relationships in their lives. When people identify unhealthy thought patterns, they can understand how their thoughts impact communication patterns and relationships. Changing harmful thought processes can enhance communication in important relationships.

In the maintenance and relapse prevention phases, the patient and clinician focus on maintaining the skills learned in the other two stages of treatment. Prevention is an essential part of any kind of recovery, even when the problem is a physical disease. With BED, CBT requires the patient and clinician to formulate a comprehensive relapse and recovery plan to help manage the negative thoughts and behaviors related to it. This involves coming up with coping mechanisms that can be used instead of binge eating during times when stress or emotional pain is at its peak. It is also a source you can refer to when you're experiencing negative thoughts and want to reframe them. Sometimes just seeing these thoughts and plans on paper make them more real to you, and that's okay. It's part of the reason for this third stage of CBT.

Hopefully, you're keeping a journal of your progress and relapses. Doing this allows you to identify triggers, yes. But it also helps you identify progress! When you're doing well or feel as if you're progressing on some level, look back at your journal and see what preceded it. Were you replacing negative thoughts with new, positive perspectives? Did communication improve an important relationship? Did specific stress or time management skills help reduce your stress levels? Whatever is enabling your progress, mark it down, and keep doing it. As you become more skilled at identifying triggers and using skills acquired by CBT to change how you react to them, urges to binge eat will decrease. You'll be able to recognize your triggers and deal with them in a healthy way before they become established negative thoughts and behavioral patterns. With CBT, the clinician positively reinforces this kind of progress as it becomes apparent.

CBT facilitates major changes, and it isn't an easy, overnight fix. It can be challenging and fraught with ups and downs, which is why we'll talk soon about what to do when you relapse (or really, really freaking want to).

Self-Actualization and BED: Life in the Pursuit of Happiness

When I suggest that you stay busy, I don't mean to fill your days with as much activity as possible to avoid what we're feeling on this inside. (This is the avoidance behavior that many of us with BED are trying to overcome). What I do mean is that I want you to fill your days with activities that make you feel happy and fulfilled, including those that involve rest or leisure time.

Maslow defined self-actualization as the desire for self-fulfillment; he said it was achieved by actualizing one's full potential. Are your current career choices emotionally satisfying and aligned with your inner purpose? For example, there are people who love helping others and feel that something is missing when they can't do so. These people often become involved in professions that allow them to express their skills at helping others. People who desire creative self-expression often feel a pervasive sense of disconnectedness with the world around them when they are not pursuing this desire on some level. They often channel it into a career when possible, or at least into a hobby that allows for self-expression and/or creativity.

My point is that we all have deep-seated desires that we must learn to express in the world. If we don't, we may never truly experience a sense of belonging or fulfillment and will feel ultimately disconnected. People tend to fill this kind of void and lack of control over personal happiness with all kinds of addictive behaviors, including those related to food.

CBT helps patients discover their inner wants and needs and find realistic ways for them to fulfill them.

What do you most enjoy doing, and how can you find ways to fit these activities into your life? If you're not someone who can or desires to incorporate the personal need for self-actualization into the career arena, there are other ways to fulfill this. Take a class for enjoyment and connect with others who share your passion or interest. This could even lead to net-working and opportunities to do what you love on some professional scale, even if it doesn't become a main source of income. Living a life that is personally satisfying is integral to good health and BED recovery. When you're doing things you love with your life and enjoying healthy personal relationships, it builds self-esteem. Feelings of emotional fulfillment and self-satisfaction greatly reduce cravings and the urge to binge eat.

When You're Tempted to Binge

Throughout your recovery process, there will be times when the urge to binge eat is strong. That's why I'm here to help you create an inner and outer support system to rely on when the urges are strong. Once you've discovered several self-soothing techniques that work for you, fall back on them when you are overly stressed and the temporary oblivion of binge eating beckons. Are you able to meditate or breathe through your stress, and then problem-solve once you're in a calmer frame of mind? If your anxiety or depression is stemming from negative thoughts, you might find that your energy becomes too drained for you to think clearly. If this happens, try to take space.

Scheduling even a brief amount of time to sit with your feelings, breathe through them, or even simply do something you enjoy might relieve your cravings. When you feel a bit better, try reframing your negative thoughts in a positive light. Again, this isn't about denying the negativity that exists in your life; there is no such thing as a human being without any negativity. It's also not about avoiding or escaping from negative situations or feelings, which many of us do when we overeat. What I'm asking you to do is very different: I just want you to sit down in a quiet place and ask your body what it needs.

As discussed earlier, the mind/ body connection is powerful and constant. When you physically feel what your body needs or connect a certain uncomfortable or painful sensation to an emotional need, you're using your intuition in a positive way. For example, some people suffer severe or migraine headaches from holding emotions inside. Others might experience chest pain and discomfort when they experience a loss or heartbreak. (Always seek professional medical help for new or persistent physical symptoms, but also keep in mind that emotions express themselves through the physical body).

Take a step back from the problem at hand, take some deep breaths, and then repeat positive affirmations in your head. If you're like I once was, you may feel tempted to hunt me down and slap me right now, but hear me out: taking space from your stress and distancing yourself from negative emotions in the moment really does help you gain a clearer perspective later on. No one can think clearly or solve problems during a fight or flight stress response; this stress response itself is designed to protect you during periods of acute stress, not help you think clearly and process emotions. When your fight or flight response has calmed down, give breathing a try. This is especially helpful when you incorporate a simple meditation into your breathing or repeat positive affirmations. Tell yourself that you are strong and capable of overcoming your urge to overeat.

Your long-term health and happiness are worth the intense struggle you are facing in the moment. It's okay to put myself first and give my body and mind what they really need right now. You should be so proud of yourself for coming this far.

Once you've figured out the emotional root of your craving and know what your body needs, go ahead and do something to address it. Take time out for yoga, meditation, or writing. Schedule a brief nap if you need one. Reach out for support from your family, friends, or therapist. There are times when you simply won't be able to overcome the urge to overeat on your own, and this is completely okay and normal. Sometimes, just venting my feelings or worries to my husband lightens the load and gives me a new, positive perspective that I would not have come up with on my own.

Whatever self-care looks like to you, do what you need to do when you're stressed and experiencing intense food cravings. That said, a lot of people think recovery is contingent on self-control and that resisting urges to overeat is the cornerstone of success. While it's true that self-control plays a significant role in recovery, exercising restraint won't be enough to help you overcome your urges on a long-term basis. Even if it works for a while, the problems you were subconsciously trying to suppress with food will resurface in other unhealthy habits or obsessions. That's why preventative care is so critical. When I refer to preventative care, I'm talking about living your life in a way that decreases stress and increases self-love, self-care, and emotional fulfillment. I'm talking about eating for both nutrition and satisfaction, not depriving yourself in the name of self-control.

Again, identify the trigger for your urge to binge eat. If it's an emotional problem that needs to be dealt with, figure out how to address it. Are you bored? Do something besides eating to alleviate this feeling, which can be more intense than people tend to give it credit for. Pencil an activity you love into your schedule. Although it's not discussed much, people with

BED often express happiness or joy through food as well. They celebrate by eating. Many times, people with BED subconsciously and automatically react to emotions and express themselves using food. If this is true for you, try calling a friend or family member to share in your happiness and celebrate with you.

I know we've discussed support systems at length, but let's touch on them briefly again. Choose a small group of family or friends you can rely on when you're overly stressed or tempted to binge eat. These should be positive influences who listen without judgment, remind you of how strong and capable you are, and lend emotional support. If your family and friends don't provide the kind of help you need, talk to your therapist about finding a support group for people in BED recovery. Support groups are especially helpful because while they connect you with people on a similar journey, the people in them are not so intimately involved in your life that they can't be objective. They aren't reliant on you to get their needs met in any way. Therapy is an invaluable tool in recovery from BED.

I highly recommend CBT because it gives you concrete, tangible ways to replace old thought processes with new, healthier ones. It gives you the coping skills you can rely on at any stressful point during the day. CBT helps transcend negative behaviors by giving you a sense of control over your thoughts and actions. It's a very structured sort of therapy that is very helpful in fighting disorders that involve addictions or compulsive behaviors that may persist despite traditional forms of psychotherapy. Being involved in therapy is an extremely preventative action on your part when it comes to avoiding binge eating behaviors. Therapy also provides you with objective, consistent support you can rely on in stressful moments that would otherwise have you making a beeline for the freezer.

Practical Tips

Now I'm going to give you a few practical tips to help you avoid binge eating. The first one is about the food you keep at arm's length in your home. You know by now that I'm not a proponent of restrictive diets, and I encourage you to still eat the sweets and treats you love in guilt-free moderation. But it's a good idea to buy these goodies in small quantities. If you've got large amounts of high-fat, high-sugar foods in your fridge, temptation is likely to loom large. So, buy the less healthy foods on your list in small portions. This is an exercise in self-discipline, not self-deprivation, an important distinction. When you've reached the point that you can tell yourself "no" and delay instant gratification, you know you've come very far in your treatment. But for now, these small tips can help you overcome temptation while it still strikes like lightning.

When your cravings are intense, try eating a healthy, protein-filled meal and then do some kind of exercise. I can practically hear the collective groans as I write this, but there's a method to my madness. Exercise is not only a way to take your mind off your cravings, but it also releases endorphins in your brain. The effect of these endorphins has been compared to the feeling one gets while taking morphine, so the experience can be powerful enough to take your mind off of overeating.

Once you feel as though you've made significant progress in your recovery, you might consider channeling your success into helping others who struggle with eating disorders. This not only gives you the satisfaction of "passing it forward," but it endows you with a sense of purpose that keeps you on track. Helping others with a problem you've experienced can be emotionally fulfilling, and it imbues you with direction in life.

You may be thinking, "All of this sounds great. But what happens if I binge? Does one mistake discount all my progress and render it meaningless?" The answer is a resounding no, and getting trapped in that cycle of negative thoughts can quickly induce guilt and shame. When people with BED experience guilt and shame over their behavior, the temptation to binge is often exacerbated. That's why I want to talk to you about what to do if you do binge eat and share with you how I stopped this cycle in its tracks.

What to do When You've Binged

The very first thing you need to do if you've binged is to forgive yourself. Everyone is human, and no one's path to recovery is without roadblocks. Yes, you do need to identify what triggered the binging and put a plan into place to prevent it from happening again. But you've got to do this with a mindset of patience, self-love, and self-compassion. If this isn't second nature to you yet and treating yourself with kindness and respect is still a conscious effort, that's completely okay! We are all surviving in a society that benefits from our insecurities, living, and working among media messages that tell us how we can become better than we are.

Contrary to what advertisements would have, you believe, these are not positive messages. With the help of therapy and support from family and friends, you can work to create a new value system within yourself. If you do binge eat, replace negative thoughts with positive ones. You may be thinking, "Now all of my progress is wasted- down the drain for one pint of ice cream that didn't even taste that good because I was so ashamed of eating it! Why don't I have any self-control? What the hell is wrong with me?"

Stop. I'm going to stop you in your tracks right there and interrupt with a more positive, accurate truth. Tell yourself in your own words, *I made a mis-*

take, but a single mistake does not encompass an entire journey in my life. I am feeling ashamed and depressed, but I do not have to continue to feel this way. I can identify the trigger that caused me to want to binge and process it with my therapist and someone close to me. I will find a solution to the problem that doesn't involve binge eating. I have the ability to change my thoughts from negative to positive, and this will improve my mood.

It's true. A single mistake, or even a few mistakes, do not define a recovery journey. If you've veered off track, you have the ability to step back on by identifying your triggers and dealing with them in therapy or with loved ones. Be aware of the same trap, one of the biggest obstacles in recovery from BED. If you find yourself feeling self-loathing following a binge, break the cycle by reaching out to your therapist or someone you love. Seek out a more objective, rational perspective than you have within yourself right now. Your therapist will help you replace negative thoughts about yourself and your circumstances with positive ones.

Extensive research has shown that internalized childhood shame can lead to eating disorders such as BED. We know that people with BED commonly report experiencing shame after binges. This deep-rooted cycle can be broken by processing trauma or repressed emotional pain and consciously relating to oneself with compassion. Even if you don't feel it, consciously forgive yourself, identify your trigger and reach out for help dealing with it. In this way, you can move forward and avoid the continuation of the shame cycle. In addition, maintaining this growth mindset can help you see positivity where you might have previously only seen flaws or faults. It can help you find better solutions to problems with self-esteem, issues in relationships with others, and other stressors. Broadening your perspective is an integral part of recovering from BED, so reach out for support from people who can help you see truths outside your subjective lens. It's never too late to get back on track and continue the journey. It's all about changing your thought patterns and embracing new, healthier ones that motivate you to keep going forward.

When you learn from them, mistakes are revealed as golden opportunities for growth. But first, you've got to let go of old, negative thought patterns that no longer suit you. If the shame cycle is especially hard to break for you, which it is for many BED sufferers, CBT is probably an excellent choice for you because it guides you step by step through the process of re-placing negative thought patterns with positive ones. It's so important to identify your triggers. There is powerful knowledge to be gained from figuring out the trigger for harmful behaviors such as binge eating.

Time is a precious commodity. Recovering from BED teaches us to use it wisely, setting aside time to appreciate eating. I personally love to eat alone with a book and savor each bite of the experience- there's a certain novelty that comes with this! But it's also important to enjoy mealtimes with family and friends, taking time to appreciate togetherness and the people we are enjoying food with. Eat slowly and savor the food, allowing yourself to appreciate where it came from, how it was made, and how it tastes and feels. By eating in this respectful manner, we are not only valuing our food but ourselves and our loved ones. This is a powerfully, satisfying experience that brings a feeling of fulfillment and reduces urges to binge eat.

Food should be a source of enjoyment. It becomes more so when you keep your meal plan exciting by trying new dishes and eating foods from different cultures. Don't be afraid to broaden your horizons; visit new places, eat at new restaurants when you can, and share new recipes with friends and family. Eating is also a social activity that brings people together and allows them to share new experiences. Experiencing fresh foods in a new environment can transport you into a different place or even culture; it can temporarily open you up to a new world, adding layers of satisfaction to your food.

So, if you're a little underwhelmed by healthy food choices at the moment, spice it up by trying a new seasoning or style of making it. Add enjoyment to the list of ingredients by sharing the meal with family or friends. Even when you're eating alone, you can up the excitement factor by taking a fresh sandwich or chicken salad to the park, laying down a picnic blanket and eating while watching the water, woods or the city go by. I'm a big fan of adding novelty to food by learning about where it came from and enjoying it in new contexts. When eating becomes just another thing to do on automatic, the pleasure is sapped from it, and we're always craving more. Yet, what we're craving is not food but satisfaction from eating. Remember that when you walk away from your meal feeling satisfied and fulfilled, you're much less likely to want to binge later. And that brings me to my final point: Although it's a long, sometimes very difficult process, recovery from BED is ultimately more about satisfaction, not deprivation. **It's about learning to enjoy yourself and your food.**

Author's Note

Recovery from Binge Eating Disorder is not an easy path, but it is ultimately a rewarding one. Throughout my recovery process, I built a foundation of self-love that guided my decisions about food and all other areas of life. Once I learned the emotional reasons behind my eating disorder, I found the courage to reach out for help in processing them so that they no longer kept me trapped in a cycle of overeating and shame. My desire to overcome BED inspired me to give others the knowledge they need to start their own recovery journey. I found a deeper purpose in life than I had before, which is helping others like me break their toxic relationship with food. During the recovery process, my research on causes and treatments for BED was the impetus I needed to stay on track. My greatest hope for this book is that it will provide you with the knowledge and resources you need to reach out for help and begin to heal.

Recovery doesn't mean you'll never have the urge to overeat; while some people stop experiencing urges to binge altogether, many still have them from time to time. However, recovery means that you have the tools you need to manage your cravings when they happen. About a month ago, I spent time with a friend who has struggled with being overweight all her life. She recently lost a lot of weight on an intensely restrictive diet, but she was beginning to gain it back again and was very upset about it. This isn't a friend I see often as she lives out of state, so I was really excited when she was in town for a whole weekend.

Anyway, on one of the days, we brought a picnic lunch to a beautiful nearby lake. I felt pretty cute in my new bathing suit, that is until my friend opened her mouth and said something that turned my whole upbeat mood around. She looked at me and exclaimed, "You are so brave to be wearing a bathing suit that shows so much skin. If it were me, I'd be constantly worrying about how my stomach looks when I sit down. Look at me: I'm in a one piece and two cover-ups!"

Now, believe it or not, my friend may not have meant to be offensive, at least not consciously. But misery loves company, and I think she didn't want to be suffering from body hate on her own. I can't lie. For a moment, I totally internalized her rude comment. My cheeks burned with old shame. I thought about how long I'd struggled to love my body despite its imperfections. I know that nobody is perfect, but comparing my body to other, thinner ones used to be a major trigger for binge eating. All of a sudden, it seemed like the sun disappeared behind the clouds, and a dark shadow loomed over me. All I wanted to do was cover up, make my excuses to leave and eat a big, fat lunch all by myself. I was surprised at my train of thought. It had been so long since I felt so angry at my body. I realized something else, too: sometimes my binge eating was a way of punishing myself for not being perfect.

But then something happened inside me. I don't know how to explain the sudden shift I felt right then, but I know that it was a positive one. The self-loving voice inside had become louder than the self-loathing voice. The love and respect I felt for myself, and my body drowned out my friend's tactless words. After all, it was she who was struggling with a poor body image, not me. Not anymore. My body is so much more than my weight, and health is defined by so many other factors. My friend was just projecting her own negative feelings about her weight onto me. And let's be real: I've been there. I struggled to love my body, even its imperfections, for many years. But I got there. And no ignorant comments from anyone was going to take that progress away from me.

While I was deep in thought, my friend's insistent voice broke my reverie. "If only I could lose thirty more pounds; then I might wear a bikini to the beach. But right now, I look like a beached whale." I decided right then and there to confront the issue head-on. I looked at my friend and said, "I get that you're struggling with body image issues, and believe me, I've been there. But I worked hard to get past them and love my body the way it is. When anyone makes comments about my weight, it sets me back. And I want to keep moving in a positive direction."

My friend reacted defensively, stumbling over her words, "I didn't mean anything bad by it. You know I think you're beautiful. But it's natural for women to feel self-conscious about their bodies. It wasn't an insult when I said you were brave for wearing that bathing suit. I meant that you're strong. You seem to always do what you want, no matter what other people say. You're not a people pleaser like me, you know?"

I did know. What my friend failed to see was that my confidence was hard won. It was the result of a commitment I made to relate to my body and mind with love, not self-loathing. And you can make that commitment, too. Oh, and just in case you were wondering, I didn't binge that night. I felt way too proud of my accomplishments to beat myself up for someone else's rude comments. The truth is, what my friend said that day was about her, not me. Just like I once did, my friend had internalized the unhealthy diet culture in our society. As for her comments toward me, she was projecting her own mixed, negative feelings about herself onto me. Once I understood this, it helped me move on and just enjoy my day in the sun (and the bathing suit that showed off my killer body). Yes, you heard me right. Even though my body doesn't fit the unrealistic, airbrushed ideals portrayed by the media, it's amazing and sexy in its own way. A year and a half ago, I used to roll my eyes at the cliched phrase, "Everybody is a beach body." Now, looking in the mirror at a body I love and deeply respect, I get it. When you love yourself, your beauty shines through more brightly than any curated image.

And it was a massive deal for me that I hadn't resorted to binge eating just because someone perceived my body as less than ideal. Poor body image used to be a major trigger for me. I realized that self-love can be a learned behavior. For most people with BED, it doesn't come naturally at first. You have to make a conscious decision to relate to yourself with compassion. When self-hateful thoughts run through your mind, you've got to actively replace them with positive ones. Eventually, it becomes a deeply ingrained habit, and your feelings about yourself shift. Self-love eventually replaced self-hatred. If that could happen for me, it could happen for you.

I began this book by asking you to make a commitment to yourself and your recovery. That's the first step. Now that the book has come full circle, I am closing with the same reminder: Change can only happen if you commit fully to yourself and your recovery. It's not an easy road. The bigger picture doesn't reveal itself all at once, instead recovery happens in steps. Sometimes you take one step forward and two steps backward. That's okay. It doesn't mean you've lost your way; it just means that you're human, just like me.

My life is very different than it was before I started my recovery journey. My relationships are more honest and fulfilling; I've learned how to meet my own needs and not get them filled by others. My relationship with food is no longer toxic and destructive but healthy and satisfying.

My life after recovery is not perfect, and I won't make any false promises that yours will be, either. But it will be filled with joy and wonder and thankfulness for the supposedly "little things" that we lose sight of when any addiction rules our lives. Now that I've used cognitive behavioral therapy to learn other ways to cope with stress and get my emotional needs met, the joy of food has been restored for me. The joy of living has, too. Looking back, I realize that I never felt truly free before my recovery from BED. I lived for the temporary feeling of control that binge eating gave me when the rest of my life felt out of my hands. But the relief was only temporary. The truth is that food controlled me, not the other way around. When I was able to figure out why, I could start changing it with the help and support of my therapist, medical doctors, and loved ones.

These days, when life gets difficult, I have the coping skills, support system, and resiliency I need to manage stress in healthy ways. I maintain a healthy relationship with food. Through my recovery and relationships with my therapist, doctors, and connections with others struggling with BED, I've discovered a new purpose in life: providing others with support in their recovery from Binge Eating Disorder. This calling has given new meaning to my life, and helping others stay on track has helped me adhere to the path of recovery even during difficult periods of my life.

One of the most important realizations I've gleaned from the recovery process is that being emotional is part of being human. You may be reading this and saying inwardly, "Well, yeah, you don't have to read a self-help book to find that out." But what I mean is that our society tends to focus on perfection, so we get caught up in the shiny images we see on social media and TV. Everywhere we look are curated images of people supposedly having the perfect relationships, traveling to beautiful, exotic places and advancing their careers. Yet, most of us have a tendency to show the world our best moments and keep the worst to ourselves.

So, you don't necessarily see that successful model or actress struggling to keep smiling for the camera despite a painful break-up or loss of a loved one. You don't necessarily see that successful entrepreneur's insecurities or tendency to binge eat when her life gets so busy, there's no time left over to take care of herself. I could go on and on listing hypothetical examples, but you get the point.

As I recovered from BED, I made an absolute decision to be someone who is "real" when sharing my recovery to a large audience. By authentically sharing both my ups and downs —my confidence and insecurity, my joy and pain—I hope to give others struggling with BED a realistic picture of what recovery looks like. Because in real life, recovery means going to both ends of the spectrum. It means embracing the polar extremes of emotion that swing like a pendulum during that first, most painful part of recovery —the period when we look at what we are versus what we'd like to be and take the first step toward closing that gap. During and after the process, we all look for role models in recovery from any mental or medical disorder.

Not everyone wants to share their struggle or recovery process, and that's totally okay! Recovery looks different for everyone, and a significant part of it is honoring your own unique process as well as that of others. I wrote this book for anyone struggling with BED, and there are no exceptions. Every part of your struggle and healing is brave and authentically yours.

When it comes to people who do choose to share, I am happy to have discovered that more and more body positive influencers are emerging on social media. Many people are showing their raw struggles with issues like depression, bipolar, eating disorders, and other personal problems. By living authentically in the public eye to varying degrees, a large population of influencers and everyday people on social media are giving others realistic role models in recovery – ones they can actually relate to and glean knowledge and inspiration from. (In fact, many popular influencers gained recognition by simply *being* everyday people in front of a large audience). I've learned so much not only from the team of mental and medical health professionals who guided me through recovery but also from others who have shared their struggles with BED. When finding support on social media, we need to be discerning. It can be a good idea to question some of our online influences and ask ourselves what it is we are drawn to about this person. But there is a lot of support to be found online if we are observant and "follow" or "friend" people who represent the parts of recovery we would like to embrace.

I could go on all day about what recovery looked like for me. But it can look different for you, and that's the beauty of it. Once you find out what recovery means to you, commit to it and don't look back.

If you struggle with BED, you know that the high or relief provided by binge eating is temporary.

It's like putting a Band-Aid over a deep, open wound. There is a much deeper, lasting happiness to be gained from loving ourselves and sharing ourselves in relationships with people who care for and support us. That's why I choose recovery every day. Every. Single. Day.

You can make the same choice. By choosing recovery over old habits, you are not just choosing recovery; you are choosing yourself, over and over again. Remember that your body is in constant, complex communication with your brain. When you send your body messages of self-love, don't think it goes unreceived. Your body responds to self-love and positive thinking by chemically shifting toward more complete homeostasis. In many ways, when you love your body, it loves you back.

Ultimately, recovery from Binge Eating Disorder is a goal, but it's also a lifestyle. Recovered from BED doesn't have to mean that you never get urges anymore, and it certainly doesn't mean that life doesn't have its share of ups and downs.

What it means is that you can manage your urges in healthy ways without giving into them. This gets easier over time. I want you to know that you can recover from Binge Eating Disorder with enough time and effort. I did it, and I believe that you can, too.

What Did You Think?

First of all, I want to say thank you for reading my book! For me, this was not just a book but a personal account of my own journey to recovery. Yet sharing my own experience was only part of my dream for this book. I also felt a strong calling to help countless others with it, and you helped make that dream a reality.

I hope this book will not only guide you through your recovery process but will also add value and quality to your daily life. If so, feel free to share this book with your friends and family by posting to Facebook and Twitter. Because Binge Eating Disorder is still poorly understood, sharing books like mine helps spread the knowledge needed for recovery.

If you enjoyed this book and found some benefit in reading it, I'd love to hear from you! If you could take some time to post a review on Amazon, it would be much appreciated. My goal as an author is to develop an interactive relationship with my readers. I value your thoughts, feelings, and ideas very much. Your feedback and support will help me to improve upon my writing craft for future projects- and make the next book even better.

All you have to do is head to Amazon.com and write a quick review to share your thoughts and feedback on this book. I hope to hear from you and wish you all the best in your future. Remember, you've got this!

10965665R00081

Made in the USA
Monee, IL
04 September 2019